Award-winning comedian Jeff Green is one of the most popular comics working in the UK today. He has staged several sell-out tours in the West End and throughout Britain and Australia. He appears regularly on television shows such as *Never Mind the Buzzcocks* and *Have I Got News For You*, and has starred in several TV specials of his own. He lives in London (alone).

For more information on Jeff Green visit *www.jeffgreen.co.uk* and *www.offthekerb.co.uk*

Also by Jeff Green

The A–Z of Living Together

JEFF GREEN

The A–Z of
Being Single

A Survival Guide to Dating and Mating
(and those lovely periods in between . . .)

timewarner
paperbacks

A *Time Warner* Paperback

First published in Great Britain by
Time Warner Paperbacks in 2003

Copyright © Jeff Green, 2003

The moral right of the author has been asserted.

A CIP catalogue record for this book is available
from the British Library.

ISBN 0 7515 3549 4

Typeset in Berkeley by M Rules
Printed and bound in Great Britain by
Clays Ltd, St Ives plc

Time Warner Paperbacks
An imprint of
Time Warner Books UK
Brettenham House
Lancaster Place
London WC2E 7EN

www.TimeWarnerBooks.co.uk

For my brothers and sisters

'Here's to woman! Would that we could fall into her arms without falling into her hands!'

AMBROSE BIERCE

'I think, therefore I'm single'

LIZZ WINSTEAD

Introduction

Hello, and welcome to the wonderful world of Singledom!

We've all been single at some point in our lives. Anyone who says otherwise is either lying, or they met their childhood sweetheart in double maths and never looked back – and where's the fun in that?

If you follow the advice in this book you'll discover that looking for love – as opposed to finding it and settling down for a life of psychological warfare on the couch (see *The A–Z of Living Together*) – can be the most exciting time of your life.

Of course the term 'single' covers a number of different circumstances.

You might be what I would call 'happily single', namely a long-term singleton, comfortably clearing the hurdles of 'table for one in a draught, please' and extra hot-water bottles in winter while enjoying the unique pleasures of sleeping in the starfish position and being able to break wind without having to blame the cat. If you fit this description, then you'll find plenty of hints and tips in this book to help you stay that way.

Or perhaps you're in a relationship that's actually going

rather well. (These things happen.) In which case, this book can help you too. How? By showing you plenty of sobering details of what life would be like if – god forbid – you messed up and lost that special someone who knows just how you like your jim-jams ironed.

If you are a 'reluctant single', reading this book with a newly broken heart and wondering how long the tears, production of copious snot and disturbing affinity with Celine Dion lyrics will last, then this book is DEFINITELY for you. It will teach you how to put it all behind you so you can move on smoothly to the next loser who runs off with all your money and sleeps with your best friend. (Fido, how could you?)

Whoever you are, this book is here to show you that being single is FUN. It's the fun of dating; mating; first kisses; breaking up, making up and being stood up; those heavenly romantic evenings and nights of passion as well as those not-so-heavenly evenings weeping into your Kentucky Fried Chicken at 2 a.m. when it all goes wrong.

Being single is the fun of living solo, which means FREEDOM – freedom you've only dreamed about. For women – how about sitting in the bath for forty-two hours if you want? Having the heating on and the windows open and not hearing a word of complaint? Imagine a world of candles and kittens. A new world. Your world. How does it feel? Good?

For men, single living means freedom for you, too – freedom to sleep in your clothes, sleep directly on the mattress, even sleep in the car if you want. It's *your* life. Do it your way. It's the freedom to finally relax in a world where no one tells you when to come home, what to wear or how many times you can reheat Chinese food. It's the freedom to have the toilet seat up, down or (my favourite) completely off its hinges. Feeling giddy?

I should point out that while I am writing from a man's point of view, I don't believe that either sex has the monopoly on the pleasures and pains of dating and the single life. This book aims to help everyone out there, happily single, reluctantly solo, already in love or looking for love, hoping to find that special someone who, one day, will want to cut all your clothes up and involve you in very expensive legal problems. Or stay with you forever.

Happy hunting. I hope you enjoy this book, near, far, wherever you are, I believe that the heart will go on . . . Oh, shut up, Celine. But then again, it's so relevant to *me* . . . (sniff). Could someone pass me a tissue?

Jeff Green

The A–Z of
Being Single

Alcohol (*see also* Confidence-building)

The industrial consumption of alcohol is one of the greatest aids to finding a new partner (or, indeed, getting over an old one). How else would we face the daunting prospect of chatting up complete strangers in front of their cynical and protective friends? (*See* **Chaperone**.)

Tell-tale signs that you've come home alone and drunk (again):

- You wake up covered in strange bruises.
- There's a half-eaten pickled onion stuck to your back.
- Your keys are still in the front door, which is now off its hinges in the lounge.
- There's a strong smell of pee coming from the rubber plant, which is a relief because you had thought the toilet flush was broken.
- You only have one eyebrow.
- This isn't your house.

Alibis

As a single person, you will have to get used to being a walking alibi for all your less honourable coupled-up friends:

SHE: (*angrily approaching with a hairbrush-shaped weapon*) Where the hell have you been? It's three o'clock in the morning! I've been phoning all the hospitals.

HE: (*backing off*) I've been with Dave.

SHE: (*uncomprehending*) Dave? Till now? Why?

HE: (*avoiding eye contact*) You know I don't like leaving him alone in that flat now she's gone.

SHE: (*spotting an incriminating collar*) And he's wearing lipstick now, is he?

HE: Yes, it's awfully sad.

Anniversaries

If you have recently split with someone and you're looking for a fresh start, you must stop celebrating all those old, melancholic anniversaries: when you first met; when you first kissed; the first time you were arrested for a breach of the peace, etc. Why not get some fun new ones like: when you last came home before midnight; when you last cleaned up someone else's mess; when you last shaved your legs and when you last ate fruit.

Answering the phone (to an ex)

We all want our ex-partners to think that we are having a better time than they are after a break up, especially if we happen to be the unfortunate dumpee rather than the lucky dumper. Phone conversations are a good opportunity to show your ex what they're missing and maybe bring on a mild choking in the back of their throat when they realise just what they lost when they tossed away another human soul, discarded it like worthless garbage to fend for itself alone . . . (Let it go, Jeff.)

Do's and don'ts when answering the phone:
- Do wait at least five rings before answering (I know it's difficult, but do try). Then say, slightly out of breath 'Sorry, I just got in from my new erotic dancing classes.' (Make sure it's not your mum calling first.)
- Don't answer immediately as though you've been camped next to it or indeed been using it as a pillow.
- Do get some husky-voiced stranger to 'accidentally' pick up the extension and say 'Oh, sorry, I didn't know you were on a call.' When asked about their identity, reply cryptically 'Oh, you know, just . . . a friend.'
- Don't be drunk (at least not before 9.30 a.m.).
- Do play happy party music in the background, as if holding an Ann Summers party, because hey, you've moved on (men: this might be difficult). For extra authenticity shout over your shoulder 'Be careful, you'll have someone's eye out with that' and, 'that'll make your eyes water, Gertrude.'

- Don't have 'Stay with me Baby', 'I Will Survive' or 'The Funeral March' playing in the background.
- Do take the whimper out of your voice.
- Don't allow your ferociously loyal friend to snatch the phone from you and shout: 'Are you happy now, you swine? You've hurt this wonderful person really badly. She wouldn't go back out with you now if you begged her. (Pause.) Probably.'

Anxiety (Sexual)

If you are anxious about your sexual abilities don't worry, you are not alone. We all have the same fears. This is why, after sex, men ask questions like 'Was I okay?' 'Did you orgasm?' and 'Do you take Visa?'

Reassuringly, women reveal their sexual anxieties in a similar way, with questions like 'Was I passionate enough?' 'Was I too forward?' and 'Do you have any other pizzas to deliver in the area?'

Arguments (*see also* Talking to yourself)

The great thing about living alone is there are no more petty arguments about who makes the tea in the morning (it's you), who left all the washing up (you did) and why you can't vacuum the toilet (you can).

B

Bad sex

If you're single and have managed to become sexually active (okay, you can stop skipping about, punching the air and hugging strangers) I'm afraid that from time to time you will experience the odd bit of bad sex. This may have something to do with you, of course, but I wouldn't worry about that too much: the important thing is that you're getting back in the community.

The great thing about being a crap shag is you never have to worry about how to end the relationship. They've usually walked out long before it ever gets to that stage. Every cloud.

Am I a crap shag? Try this simple test:
Him:

- The local brothel won't return your calls   20pts
- It always seems to be 'that time of the month'   15pts
- Your premature 'accidents' are greeted with high fives   15pts
- When you ask 'How was that?' she replies 'How was what?   5pts

- Your post-coital routine consists of rolling off, removing your socks and saying 'Sorry love, that's never happened to me before'   10pts
- Her new night attire is comprised of pyjamas, nightdress, duffel coat, oven gloves, surgical tights and a large sign around her neck saying 'Bugger off'   15pts

Her:
- You feel the need to ask *him* whether he managed to achieve orgasm   5pts
- You think the *Karma Sutra* comes with pilau rice   10pts
- You get sued by a local missionary couple for defamation of character   20pts
- He doesn't seem in any rush to fix the bedroom light   5pts
- None of his friends come on to you when he's not around   15pts
- He manages to fall into a suspiciously deep sleep (from which he can't be roused) in the time it takes you to take your tights off   25pts

Beater

A socially unskilled friend who comes along with you on the pull for the sole purpose of driving any available women into your range. As in:

You and the 'beater' enter a bar and buy a couple of drinks.
You move over to the fruit machine near the exit while the
beater circles the bar. You begin to hear the growing sound of
distressed female voices. Soon a couple of women approach
you at speed and settle near the machine.

SHE1: Do you mind if we stand over here? There's a
right prat knocking about over there.

YOU: (*feigning disinterest*) No problem. (*Looking over*)
Yeah, he looks a bit of an idiot. (*Then, with sly
nonchalance*) So, what are you two girls doing this
evening?

SHE2: We were going to stay here, but not if that tosser's
going to stick around.

YOU: It looks like he might. (*Then, as if a light bulb has
just come on*) Hey, why don't you come to this new
place I know just round the corner?

SHE1: (*seeing the beater approaching*) Why not, let's go.
Quick.
(*And reload*)

Being stood up

This is shoddy behaviour, only marginally less reprehens-
ible than turning up for the evening with a second date
(you know who you are).

TIP Try to retain some dignity. You will be exposed to
ridicule if you are seen outside the cinema:

- Constantly looking at your watch in puzzlement whilst holding a bouquet of limp flowers like an Olympic torch.
- Looking expectantly into the eyes of every passing female, like a tied up Labrador waiting for its owner to come out of a sweetshop.
- Shivering.
- Banging your head against the wall, wailing 'Why does this always happen to me?'
- Still there the next day.

Beauty tips

If you are hoping to make an elegant splash in the singles market rather than an undignified belly flop, then you will have to make an effort with your appearance. Don't worry. Feel free to use these sure-fire beauty tips to give you the edge in the competitive world of the singleton:

Beauty tip FAQs
- How can I look twenty years younger? *Stand further away.*
- How can I get that expressionless, frozen 'Botox' look on the cheap? *Shave off your eyebrows. (Or get drunk twice.)*
- Have I had too many facelifts? *If you now have a curly, triangular beard, then yes.*
- My dream is to look like Barbie. What's the most expensive operation? *Getting your head to turn all the way around.*

- I want the best smile on the beach. What should I do? *Move to Eastern Europe.*
- I'm going to a party. How can I make my eyes sparkle instantly? *Rip a few nose hairs out before making your entrance.*

Blind dates

Don't forget to feed the dog.

Bondage (for beginners)

One of those bedroom 'fantasy' games played during the first flush of a relationship (*see also* **Belly Raspberries**, **Strip Poker**, '**Find the Flake**', etc.). The cold reality is you, blindfolded and naked, tied to your **futon** by your dressing-gown cord, scout belt, old school tie and a frayed bicycle bungee (stop me if I get too sophisticated), feeling embarrassed and vulnerable, hoping that this wasn't all just a prelude to the real game of 'Happy birthday. Surprise, surprise!' or 'So, what's it to be? The nipple clamps or your PIN number?'

Boomerangs

A traditional instrument used to spoil a kangaroo's afternoon (should you so wish). Also the modern term to describe those strange individuals who in adulthood actually *choose* to live with their parents.

Does he still live with his mum? Ways to spot if he's a homing pigeon:

- He has pin-sharp creases down the front of his under-pants.
- He never seems to be short of a sugared almond.
- You take him to a nightclub and the UV lighting reveals that he has a bright white square of 'Bounce' stuck to his back.
- He's not allowed to receive phone calls during *Casualty*.
- He smells vaguely of scones.

Does she still live with her mum?

- She puts her fingers in her ears when she walks past Mothercare, and doesn't seem to want to go home at night.

That pretty much covers it.

Boring the pants off your friends

If you have been chucked recently, you may be frustrated by how little time you get to sound off to your friends about how awful you are feeling. Even worse, if you've been miserable for a while, you may even have noticed that no one greets you with the customary 'How are you?' anymore. In this situation, let go of the embarrassment associated with extreme self-absorption and look for any opportunity to swing the conversation round to your predicament. It's important for your own healing process and anyway, you can always get new friends.

TIP Why not try this Trojan horse conversational gambit?

YOU: I'm thinking of changing my phone.

FRIEND: Why, what's wrong with the one you've got?

YOU: Because SHE never bothers to call me on it that's why.

FRIEND: (*weary*) Hasn't she called you, then?

YOU: Of course not. Do you know the last time she actually called *me . . .?* (*and you're off!*)

Or how about:

YOU: (*innocuously*) How much are kippers these days?

FRIEND: Kippers? I've no idea. What do you want to buy kippers for?

YOU: Because I'm thinking of putting some behind HER radiator when I go round to collect my stuff.

FRIEND: (*tricked and dejected*) Why, what's happened this time?

YOU: Well. (*Settling in for a long moan.*) You remember what she said to me the last time I phoned her . . . (*and away you go*).

Or why not try this wrong footer:

YOU: I've got a new girlfriend!

FRIEND: (*relieved*) That's great. What's she like?

YOU: Nothing like HER (. . . *and you're in. Seamless.*)

Budget dating (*see also* Zoos)

Until you are certain about the true depths of your feelings for someone, and have satisfied any niggling doubts (*see* **Psychopaths**, **Ice-maidens**, etc.) it is always prudent to limit your 'spend' on them. The following are excellent dates for the limited pocket:

- The library. What could be more romantic than snuggling up together to read those riveting local disability newsletters, and playing with the microfiche (up to eight o'clock on a Wednesday)? And if your partner is getting on your nerves, you can simply say: 'Shhhh.' Perfect.
- Construction sites. Why not spend an evening peering through that peep-hole in the wooden perimeter fence cut just for the purpose, and watch cement dry under the stars.
- An evening at your mum's house. Lots (and I mean *lots*) of nice food as well as an invaluable, free lesson for all present in how a man like you *should* be treated.
- Anywhere. Just remember to say 'I'll meet you <u>in</u> there.'

C

Car insurance

If you're a single woman, you will be pleasantly surprised by the nice low rates. If you're a single man, you will be wondering why you're being asked to pay the national debt of Kazakhstan. Still, at least the breakdown services come to you first. Oh sorry, my mistake.

Carrier bags

One of the mysteries of modern life is that no matter how hard you try, you will not pull a woman if you're carrying stuff in a plastic bag at the time. (*See also* **Food in your teeth**, **Dandruff on your glasses**, etc.)

Chaperone (a.k.a. the Guard dog)

Ubiquitous friend who, flushed with her promotion from coat minder and chewing-gum dispenser, sticks to your intended squeeze like glue, pouring scorn on any stories/lies you tell in your entirely innocent attempt to trick your way into her friend's affections (sexual).

TIP Could possibly be neutralised by your Beater.

Chatting someone up (*see also* Alcohol, The art of telling lies, etc.)

Perhaps the most challenging and nerve-racking aspect of being single is the chat-up scenario.

FRIEND: Okay, you have two choices. Chat up that pretty girl over there, or be parachuted naked into Leicester Square. What's it to be?

YOU: Well, you know, I could do with the fresh air.

What you need in all cold chat-up situations (when you can't count on looks, fame or bribery) are some good quality introduction lines. Although stock chat-up lines have acquired something of a cheesy reputation recently, with a bit of ingenuity it is possible to breathe new life into some familiar material:

Chat-up lines for younger lovers:
- So, do you want to come and blow some confirmation money?
- Hey, nice dental braces – wanna hook up some time?
- Can I have a photo of you so Santa knows what to bring me for Christmas? (I write every year.)
- I know this really amazing bike shed that's just opened – shall I see if I can get us a reservation?

Chat-up lines for older lovers:

- Is that a hernia in your pocket or are you just pleased to see me?
- Did you break a hip when you fell from heaven?
- Get your cardigan, sweetheart, you've pulled.
- Is it cold out or are you smuggling tic tacs in your socks? (Don't forget to duck with this one.)
- Hi cutie – do I come here often?

Competitiveness

When it comes to getting the best out of your sexual performance, you may find that some women are not averse to exploiting your natural competitiveness in the bedroom.

You are both in bed, mid-coitus (well, a few seconds in, anyway).

YOU: (*puff*) Oh yeah (*wheeze*), I think I'm nearly there. Are you? (*splutter*)

SHE: Not quite.

YOU: Okay (*gasp*). What's your ETA? (*croak*)

SHE: (*sensing this might be over a little quicker than she had hoped*) Soon, I guess. (*Then thinking of a plan*) Look, I don't know if I should tell you this . . .

YOU: (*alarmed*) What? I'm not losing my hair am I? (*You check to see if there is a mirror behind you.*)

SHE: No. It's, well . . . (*coyly*) I've never had an orgasm before.

YOU: (*suddenly very interested*) Really?

SHE: It's silly, isn't it?

YOU: (*taking the bait*) No, it's not silly. It's a shame though, cos they're quite good.

SHE: (*disingenuously*) I've heard that. And of course I'd like to try one, especially with you. It's just, well, no one's ever managed it with me. If you did, you'd be the first. (*Then softly, in your ear*) Ever.

YOU: The first, eh? (*You allow yourself a moment to imagine the accolades you might receive from her girlfriends, possibly even a mention in the local paper.*) Well then, I think you'd better just wait there.

You quickly slip on your pants (there's no point scaring your pets or the neighbours) and get up to leave.

SHE: (*smiling to herself – the plan is working*) Where are you going?

YOU: (*quietly relishing the challenge*) To the attic, to get my stuff.

You arrive back covered in fibreglass dust, wearing a Batman outfit and brandishing what looks like a food mixer.

YOU: Okay lady, let the dog see the rabbit (*or words to that effect*).

We hear the sound of a motor being revved up, followed by some saucy giggling.

Several HOURS later.

YOU: (*near to death and rapidly losing interest*) Bloody hell, love. Hasn't it happened yet?

SHE: (*with demonic focus*) I'm teetering on the edge.

YOU: (*impatiently*) Well fall over it then.

SHE: Don't rush me.

YOU: Rush you? Have you seen the time? I've got work in an hour. One of my arms has gone numb, I've got chapped lips and . . . oh god, look at my hands! (*You offer up a couple of deformed claws.*) I'll never play the piano again.

SHE: (*taking great offence*) Well, if it's too much trouble for you, let's just forget about it.

In a huff she turns off the Sade CD (see later), blows out the 'romantic' candles and rolls over. In the gloom we see you, sitting on the edge of the bed, head bowed in defeat, slowly taking off your Batman cape. Secretly you hope she doesn't tell her girlfriends about your failure.

A few seconds later. In the darkness:

SHE: (*big sigh*) What a shame. I really thought you were going to be the one.

YOU: (*defensive and ashamed*) Yeah well . . .

A few more seconds later.

YOU: So how close were you?

SHE: Very.

YOU: Okay. I'll give it one last go.

We hear the sound of a match being struck – the candle is re-lit. Click – the musical greyness is back: '. . .your love is king, you crown me with your heart . . .'

YOU: You'd better pass me my lip balm and my scuba gear. But you can phone in sick for me. And do you mind not gripping so hard on my ears this time?

We hear the sound of the motor again and more self-satisfied giggling. Fade to black.

Confidence

In the event of a damaging split-up, it is very important that you get your self-confidence back as soon as possible (*see* **Wonder bras**, **Vertical-striped clothing** and **Superman pyjamas**, etc.). This can be achieved in several different ways: embarrassing role-playing exercises, expensive therapy sessions or from rapidly downing half a bottle of cheap Grappa. The choice is yours.

Customer comment cards

If you keep being dumped you may want to find out why you are repulsing people with monotonous regularity. A good marketing tool used by many cutting-edge companies (and the rail networks) to obtain feedback is the Customer Comment Card. Why not create your own and ask that fast-exiting weeping/screaming/violent/worn down/nervous wreck/psychotic (delete as applicable) partner to fill it in? This way you might improve the service you give to future (it doesn't hurt to be optimistic) girlfriends:

1) How would you describe your overall experience of dating me?
   ☐ A wonderful, heart-warming experience that has left you with renewed faith in the inherent beauty and kindness of humanity.
   ☐ A not unpleasant time but with enough niggling doubts to leave you knowing it's not for you.
   ☐ Awful, leaving you with a disturbing desire to do me or anyone who even looks like me harm.
   ☐ Emotionally scarring and regressive.

2) Did I compliment you
   ☐ Regularly.
   ☐ Now and again.
   ☐ When I wanted a favour.
   ☐ When I wanted a sexual favour.

3) How was my general level of hygiene?
   ☐ Poor.
   ☐ Very poor.
   ☐ Piss poor.
   ☐ An insult to tramps.

4) What was the overall quality of gifts given during our relationship?

☐ Okay – you particularly remember a fine Cornish pasty I gave you last Christmas.

☐ Not bad – although you could have done without the six months' prison sentence for handling stolen goods.

☐ You don't recall – you burned everything I ever gave you.

☐ There were no gifts.

5) When saying 'I love you', did I

☐ Say it and mean it?

☐ Say it but only when prompted?

☐ Say it but only when threatened with violence and a ban on conjugal relations?

☐ Okay, I never said it.

6) How long did we play 'No, you put the phone down first'?

☐ 1 day

☐ 1 week

☐ 1 month

☐ Until the arrival of the first phone bill

7) Once we had engaged in sexual activity, did my enthusiasm for our relationship

    ☐ Grow stronger and more committed as if our physical union was a perfect demonstration of our love for each other?

    ☐ Stay the same except for the odd argument over condom disposal?

    ☐ Pretty much fizzle out as if, oddly, I was only really after getting my leg over?

    ☐ You're sorry but your counsellor has asked you not to recall such memories outside of a proper therapy environment.

8) How would you describe my foreplay technique?

    ☐ Like a concert pianist playing a beautiful Steinway.

    ☐ Like a drunken pub musician banging away at a clapped-out old upright.

    ☐ A disturbing variation on the Heimlich Manoeuvre.

    ☐ You missed it while blinking.

9) With regard to sex, did you have to

    ☐ Beat me off with a stick.

    ☐ Beat me off and then use the stick.

    ☐ Induce me with offers of dirty talk and pizza.

    ☐ Get me going with a couple of Red Bulls, Viagra and a car battery.

10) What was your general satisfaction level with my genitals?

- [ ] Not bad, but I'd get that kink looked at.
- [ ] Okay – they looked like genitals only smaller.
- [ ] They wouldn't win a beauty contest.
- [ ] What genitals?

11) What did you think of the quality of my lavatory?
- [ ] Good. It's nice to find a man who keeps his well vacuumed.
- [ ] Passable, so long as you treat it like rock climbing, i.e. don't look down.
- [ ] Gross. Do you have a single hair left on your body?
- [ ] Primitive. I thought we'd moved on from a wooden bucket and a sponge on a stick.

12) How would you describe the chances of us getting back together again?
- [ ] Okay. You're kind of cute and you don't smell too awful.
- [ ] I'm sorry, I've just been diagnosed with Obsessive Compulsive Disorder and will be washing my hair for the rest of my life.
- [ ] I'd rather eat my own young.
- [ ] Forget it. If I'm ever seen with you again, I've asked my friends to kill me.

- [ ] From time to time I may sink so low as to make your personal information available to other utterly unsuitable men. Please tick the box if you do not wish to be contacted by a procession of sad and pathetic commitment-phobes in search of cheap thrills from anything with a pulse.

Female customer comment card:

1. Did I agree with you enough?
   Yes/no
2. Was I naked enough?
   Yes/no

Thank you for your time.

D

Danger

Women have always been attracted to men of danger. (In fact, they're not averse to a few thrill-seeking acts of their own. Note the way they push the seat forward when they drive, so their face is half an inch from the windscreen – no room for error, you see.) So it follows that if you want to be irresistible to the opposite sex, you should think about ways to come across as 'mad, bad and dangerous to know'. Consider:

- Setting the alarm on your digital clock using only the 'fast' button.
- Wearing leather-soled shoes in icy conditions.
- Having only a 'little' knowledge.
- Snuffing out candles without licking your fingers first.
- Sporting checks with stripes.
- Returning to an unlit firework (on 6 November).
- Swallowing your chewing gum.
- Licking a battery seductively (but not from a car).

If all else fails just emit some random low growling.

Dating agencies (*see also* Personal ads)

Undoubtedly a convenient way for busy people to find partners (*see also* **Supermarkets**, **Badminton clubs**, **Blow-up doll shops**, etc.) but you can't help thinking they're a bit like going fishing at a trout farm. Sure, you'll catch a fish – but where's the sport?

Desperation

If you are out on the pull after a break-up, seeking a quick ego fix to help soothe your bruised soul, you may discover that some people (women) have annoying, inbuilt antennae that can detect who is passing through Loserville and who isn't. Luckily for women, men don't have this radar (or, to be honest, they don't bother switching it on) and have no problem pursuing the emotionally vulnerable and psychologically damaged (after a few drinks anyway). (*See also* **Emergency human contact**, **Pulling (on your own)**, etc.)

Tell-tale signs that you're becoming too *desperate:*
- You wait at airports with a sign saying 'Anyone'.
- You start a conga line at a funeral.
- You board packed tube trains wearing a home-made Velcro suit.
- Some of your recent movements could be described as 'lurking'.
- You're overheard at a party uttering the plea: 'Oh please, I'll be really quick.'

- You start thinking seriously about following up some of your mum's dating suggestions.

Dinner parties

While there is always the risk that some people won't leave when you want them to – like just after they've handed over the wine – it is still worth throwing the odd dinner party at home. After all, now you're single no one's going to ask you to any of theirs. ('Boy, girl, boy, girl, boy, girl, boy, boy— oh. Do we have to invite him?') The upper and middle classes have long recognised that these gatherings are a 'super' way to meet the opposite sex in an un-pressured, convivial, 'squiffy'* environment.

Other ways to become middle class:
- Trim the crusts off your chip butties and cut them into triangles.
- Get the *Big Issue* delivered.
- Serve Pot Noodle on a plate.
- Grow a beard.
- Decide that you're quite looking forward to one of your children turning out gay.
- Lament the demise of the red squirrel.
- Lose the ability to dance well to pop music.
- Feel guilty about . . . *everything* (but especially the squirrels).

*pissed

TIP When a woman says she's looking for something more from a relationship than just dinner and sex, don't say 'Okay. How about a large brandy?'

Dogs

Lonely? 'Why not get a dog?' they say. Very good advice, although it must be said that no matter how many obedience classes you send them to, they never really get the hang of making a good chilli con carne, and it can be highly embarrassing to go to a house party only to be told that your 'date' has been caught drinking out of the toilet bowl and dragging her arse across the living room carpet. Still, what a kisser! (*See* **Pash rash**, **XXXs**)

Double dating

If, when you go to restaurants, you always fancy what everyone else is having rather than what you ordered, then double dating might not be for you.

Dressing gowns

An essential item of clothing for those dying days of the relationship, when you spend most of your evenings standing in the street shouting phrases like: 'Go to your fancy woman then, see if she'll cook your dirty pants and wash your dinner. Hang on, that's not right. All right, bugger off. You'll be back', and 'No, I will not get out of the way. You will stay here and talk about it. (*Then, clutching at straws*) Look, you can't drive in your slippers', until a couple of squad cars arrive (*see* **Anniversaries**).

Types of dressing gowns:
His: Only one – towelling material with multiple, attractive pulled threads – bought for him by his mum when he was eighteen to take to college and which now barely covers his scrotum. Thinks it is self-cleaning.

Hers: Several different styles. Quality depends on how far down the I'm-Finished-With-Men Road she has travelled. Of particular note is the combined nylon dressing gown/Van der Graff generator, able to create enough static electricity from the fluff around the collar and cuffs to stun a small mammal. Doesn't quite go with those favourite shabby Goofy head slippers.

Dutch

Multilingual yet obviously tight-fisted nation who insist on their womenfolk paying half for everything.

E

Eating (alone)

If you are going to eat alone then my advice is: do it in the privacy of your own home. Don't give waiters the pleasure of rubbing in your no-partner shame by deliberately gathering up the cutlery, glasses and napkins from the other place settings (as if it's your kleptomania that's putting people off), snuffing out the candle (no romance for you tonight) and dragging your table towards the dark recesses of the restaurant (for fear that your 'loser aura' might affect their fragile ambience).

> **TIP 1** If you find you are being maltreated in a restaurant, simply get out a pad of paper and start making overtly secretive notes. Then, when (or should I say, if) a waiter passes by, ask innocently: 'Excuse me, is "overpriced" hyphenated?' and 'Which would you say would look snappier in print – "unappetizing puke" or "reheated vomit"?'

> **TIP 2** In restaurants like these – don't.

Elasticated sheets

A marvellous invention (but how do you fold them?) which for the single person ranks alongside penicillin, Jammy Dodgers (the winning combination of a friendly face and a tasty snack) and late-night radio phone-ins as one of modern society's finest achievements. Bring on the Electric Duvet Changer, Self-Holding Ladder and All Day Christmas Dinner In A Can.

E-mail

A great way to flirt with colleagues (and let's face it, it beats working). But be warned: e-mails can also be used by weirdo stalkers and disgruntled exes to make your life unpleasant. Installing an e-mail filter to scan for words like: 'know where you live', 'boil', 'isn't over till I say so', 'pet rabbit', 'found a way for us to be together forever' and 'testicles in a vice' should help solve the problem.

Emergency human contact (*see also* Desperation)

There will be times between 'liaisons' when you are so starved of human contact that you will need to find emergency substitutes.

Men, consider:
- Going through airport security covered in hidden metal objects.

- Fake-drowning at your local pool to receive a nice, big, sloppy kiss-of-life. Don't forget to pop your tongue in just as you're 'coming round'.
- Going for a bra fitting. It's your right too.
- Physiotherapy for that mystery groin strain. Higher . . . higher . . . *bingo*!
- Refereeing a game of women's rugby.
- Walking through customs after a flight from Colombia with a pronounced limp and a cheeky wink.
- Having a sex change.

Women, consider:
- Sitting alone in a sports bar in a low cut dress for five minutes.

That should pretty much do it.

Emergency shag

That unwitting person you rely on when you're feeling unloved and lonely to come round late at night and give you a damn good— oh, excuse me, the phone's ringing . . . but it's 2 a.m., what can *they* want?

Emotional vertigo

Term used to describe those fleeting but terrifying moments when you are stopped in your tracks by a memory of something you did that was highly embarrassing or deeply shameful, usually involving alcohol and body fluids. The vertigo is experienced when, in that split second, you see the depths of your base behaviour, go slightly dizzy and involuntarily utter the primordial sound: 'Hrrrrrgh.'

FRIEND: Right, that's the shopping nearly done. I've just got to get some bananas. Oh, and I need some baby oil.

YOU: (*going glassy-eyed and momentarily losing your balance*) Hrrrrrgh.

FRIEND: Are you okay? You've gone quite pale.

Ending the relationship

There is no easy way to let down the one you no longer love, although painstaking and selfless male research has revealed that not phoning them is reasonably hassle free.

> *50 Ways to Leave Your Lover*
> *(Or to Get Them to Leave You)*
> (with apologies to Paul Simon)

1. I'm sorry, I got hit on the head this morning. I really have no idea who you are. So I think you'd better pack your things and go.
2. The fact is, I've been living a lie – I'm gay/straight/ Danish/horrible/only 14 (delete as applicable).
3. Leave a pile of clothes on a beach with a note saying: 'Gone for a swim to relieve my leg cramps.'
4. And so you see, technically I'm a eunuch.

5. I *really* like your sister.

6. A man stopped me in the street today and told me this amazing stuff about Scientology.

7. Sorry, I can't explain now. Gotta go. I've been activated.

8. How can you be jealous of a farmyard animal?

9. I'm just going outside. I may be some time.

10. I'm not sure if it's safe for me to be in a relationship so soon after coming off my medication.

11. I've checked out our family trees and guess what? We're cousins!

12. Hey, the gimp suit's arrived.

13. Jesus wants me for a sunbeam.

14. Carry this package through customs for me, love. I'll meet you on the other side.

15. Take these paracetamol tablets for me, love. I'll meet you on the other side.

16. I'm just nipping to the shop for some milk, but please don't feel you can't move on.

17. No, your bum looks *huge* in that.

18. I love kids. I want hundreds.

19. I've decided to go on a strict diet of cabbage, real ale and pickled eggs.

20. I *really* like your brother.

21. Would it bother you if I wore a nappy around the house and called you mummy?

22. Yes, there's only a driver's airbag but as I bought the car you'll just have to take your chances.

23. I've decided I'm going to call you 'me bitch' from now on.

24. We don't need toothbrushes, eventually teeth start cleaning themselves.
25. Where do you stand on polygamy, number six?
26. You know they're watching me, don't you?
27. I *really* like your mum.
28. Could you take these antibiotics? I got a kidney infection off a toilet seat and I think I might have passed it on to you.
29. Well, that's that. I'm bankrupt.
30. From now on I'd like to be called Dolores/Bernard.
31. I'm sorry, but I must leave you now. I'm not from your world, I'm from the future.
32. You know I've always had a problem with commit-ment? Well guess what? I've been committed again.
33. Sting says, 'If you love someone set them free.' So shoo!
34. I *really* like your dad.
35. I don't think I'm being the unreasonable one. I only asked you to change three things – your looks, your friends and your personality.
36. I'd given up all hope but would you believe it, she's out of the coma.
37. You'll never take me alive, copper.
38. I'm just going upstairs for a spot of bagpipe practice.
39. Oh no, the brakes have failed. I'll try and slow it down, you jump for it. Quick, save yourself, while you've still got time.
40. Oh, come on love. It might be a kidney to you, but it's a new car to me.

41. I want to remember you just as you are now – leaving.
42. You know I said you were the woman/man of my dreams? Well, my alarm clock's just gone off.
43. I want to grow old with you. So how about we meet up in forty years' time?
44. Has my evil twin been filling your head up with nonsense again?
45. I see dead people.
46. Of course I still care about you. Didn't I promise to forward your post?
47. I know you were fast asleep at the time but I'm finding it difficult to forget what you said.
48. Now, you close your eyes while I hide.
49. I really love you. Only joking. You're chucked.
50. You are the weakest link, goodbye.

F

Failing hindsight

That odd phenomenon which occurs when you look back at an abusive and destructive relationship and think: 'You know, it wasn't that bad. I'd really like to give it another chance.'

- I know he took all my money and slept with my sister but he did buy me a Kit-Kat last February.
- Yes, she is a dangerous fantasist who burned my house down, but she had a lovely smile.
- Okay, she's doing five years for poisoning me but they *were* rice crispie chocolate crackles.
- I know he tried to garrotte me but life was never dull. And anyway, I look good in polo necks.

Fantasies

Be careful when nagging a new partner to fulfil that ultimate male fantasy of being in the company of two women (*see also* **Multi-tasking**) as one day you might have to field requests from her along the lines of: 'So . . . how about you and Trevor put on a little show for me? You know, maybe start off with a little sexy dancing together, maybe some smooching, followed by a bit of mutual back-hair rubbing . . . Come on, you like each other, don't you? You go to all those football matches together, you must have something going on.'

TIP When role-playing the popular fantasy 'Shall we pretend it's the first time we've met?', it might be prudent to keep some of your more private thoughts to yourself.

In the pub.

SHE: Do you want to play a game?

YOU: Not here, their darts are rubbish.

SHE: No, a special game. A *sexy* game.

YOU: Oh, hello?

SHE: How about we pretend that tonight's the first night we met?

YOU: Erm, all right.

SHE: Okay, we'll do it exactly how it was that evening. I'll go over to where I was sitting and you stand at the bar looking moody and mysterious. How about it?

YOU: Sure.

She walks across the pub and makes herself comfortable in a chair by the window.

Ten minutes later. You are still at the bar. She walks back over angrily.

SHE: **What's going on? You weren't even looking at me.**

YOU: **I was eyeing up your mate.**

(Fade to black and blue.)

Finding yourself

An excellent excuse for drinking heavily and not washing.

First impressions (Sixty seconds. Is that all we get?)

It is a medical fact that it takes just sixty seconds for someone to decide whether they are attracted to us. This allows just enough time to say: 'Me? Well, I'm a fully trained masseur and I own a string of very expensive ladies shoe shops' or 'I know this sounds weird but cooking and cleaning make me really horny.'

Remember though, first impressions last. Avoid:

Him:
- Lycra shorts.
- Storing cigarettes in the sleeve of your T-shirt.
- Bra twanging.
- White socks.
- Limbo dancing.

Her:

- Facial tattoos.
- Storing beer in your bra.
- Scratch and sniffing.
- Pop socks.
- Mud wrestling.

First love

That person whose memory still makes your heart beat faster and who you'd secretly go back to in a flash if there was a chance the bus shelter was still there and that she'd still show you her bra for a Curly Wurly (*see also* **Young love**).

Flabbiness

A good excuse is to call it 'winter fat'. Just don't mention it's from winter 1985 (*see also* **Gym membership**).

Where to put your belt?

If you have only recently acquired a belly you may be wondering where to put your belt. For men, belt location is a factor of age, in the same way that eye-brow height is for women. There are two standard belt-settings commonly seen on men – underneath the belly for younger guys and over the top of the belly for older men. Indeed, as you get older you will notice your belt moving further towards the sky until about the age of ninety, when there will just be a little belt at the top of your head like a halo.

Flatmates

Flatmates are great for providing introductions to new people once your usual pool of work colleagues, college pals and siblings finally wise up to your dating methods and ban you from traumatising any more of their friends.

> TIP For the lazy singleton, flatmates make the perfect date. Consider:
> - You don't have to pick them up or take them home.
> - They know the way you live and by returning your advances have implicitly accepted your behaviour in all its feet-soaking and milk-stealing glory.
> - Arguments, snoring, non-consultation re: channel hopping, general clinginess and any of your own guilt-ridden bouts of 'Oh my god, what have I started? I feel so trapped' can all be solved by simply sending them to their *own* room. And they pay rent! When will the hell end?

Flirting

We all like a good flirt. It brightens our day to think that someone out there fancies us without needing the incentive of a cash payment. According to sex-ologists (whatever *they* are, but I'll bet it looks cool on your passport), the key areas of flirting have been identified as:

Mirroring

Apparently, we are attracted to people who subconsciously mirror our own behaviour. But do you really want to go out with someone who constantly fiddles with her crotch, slyly ogles other women's breasts and likes to end most Saturday evenings with a visit to Casualty? On second thoughts . . .

> **TIP** If you intend to use mirroring as a chat-up technique, do be careful. You may find it doesn't work to your advantage if your date has a limp, a nervous twitch, fleas or is a professional sword swallower.

The Eyebrow Flash

A well-known 'tell', this internationally recognised sign is a sure-fire indication that someone is interested in you. But before acting on this signal, do check that they weren't simply looking in your direction as they sat down and discovered their thong was too tight.

Blinking

We are told that if someone fancies you, their blink-rate goes up. Or it could be that they're wearing contact lenses and you're using enough aftershave to sedate a donkey.

TIP 1 Most men cannot read the complicated signals that show a woman fancies them. (Why can't they roll up a trouser leg and give us a funny handshake, or a simple thumbs up – something we can understand?) So the next time you're out on the pull, why not invite along that particularly jealous ex-girlfriend of yours: her antennae were always second-to-none when it came to spotting any 'cheap tart' who was coming on to you.

TIP 2 It is said that women are often attracted to men who remind them of their father. So, when out on a date, remember to greet her with: 'You're not going out in that'. At the restaurant, go around turning off any unnecessary lights, saying 'What do you need all these lights on for? We're not millionaires.' In the morning (if you're lucky) don't forget to spend several minutes in the bathroom bringing up copious amounts of phlegm, question the sexual orientation of any good-looking male TV presenters and, when she asks for a lift to work, exclaim: 'What do you think I am, a bloody taxi service?' That ought to do it.

Places and occasions where flirting may be inappropriate:
- During labour (possibly not relevant to men).
- When taking part in a police line-up.
- When watching someone eat a banana.
- From a pulpit.

- At the opticians (even though s/he is looking deep into *your* eyes too).
- At an auction (unless you've got lots of spare cash).
- At a urinal (unless you're prepared to follow it through).
- When wearing loose-fitting tracksuit bottoms without underwear (possibly not relevant to women).
- When receiving a prostate examination (ditto).
- When counselling the recently bereaved.

Flirting triangle

Polite way of saying that when men fancy you they look at your breasts.

Foreplay (*see also* Zones (erogenous))

If you have just emerged from a long-term relationship, your foreplay skills may be a little rusty. (Ah yes, the clitoris. That's the thing that turns a caterpillar into a butterfly, isn't it? – *see* **A dictionary**.) But don't panic. There are ways to get round this difficult and time-consuming procedure:

Ways to get out of foreplay
- The doctor tells me it is the worst case of RSI of the tongue he has ever encountered.
- Foreplay? Surely my attractiveness alone is all the stimulation you need?
- I've got a cab waiting.
- Sorry, I'm a vegetarian.

- Well, I'm ready. Do you want to give me a nudge when you are? (Good luck with this one.)

Or you could just date for a few months, it'll soon go.

> **TIP** When attending to a partner's nipples during fore-play, try not to spoil the moment by saying: 'Wow, this is better than Etch-a-Sketch.'

Friends – *see* Boring the pants off them, Pretend boyfriend, Kiss of death, etc.

F*** off – *see* Speed dating

Fussy women

It is frustrating when you bring a date back and she won't stay the night for the feeble reason that she hasn't got any clean clothes for work in the morning. We all know that if the circumstances were reversed you would happily go to work dressed in a bin bag if you thought you were going to get fiddled with. It is equally frustrating when she can't be brought round by an offer to lend her that pair of your ex-girlfriend's old pants and tights, which you found behind the radiator covered in fluff (*see* **Uses for** . . .)

Futon

Going by the feel of these trendy beds, the Japanese word for 'concrete'.

G

Getting noticed

In today's cut-throat dating scene, it is important that you stand out from the crowd (*see* **First impressions, Where to buy a clown suit,** etc.)

> **TIP 1** If you can't afford a flashy car to attract the attention of potential mates, why not get yourself a really crap car? Say, one with only three doors, each painted a different colour, with a noisy engine belching out black noxious fumes and a broken silencer that makes it sound like a tank? Then you too can drive up and down the high street on a Saturday night, turning ladies' heads.

> **TIP 2** Women: when using the ancient art of make-up to create an impression, remember that the word here is subtle. If, when you've got your war paint on, you look like you are auditioning for the role of lead singer in a tribute band to The Cure, then you may want to think about getting some professional guidance.

Glitter

There is always something slightly unhinged about people who wear this stuff not as a fleeting fashion statement but as a lifestyle (*see also* **Mad girlfriends**).

> **TIP** Exercise care when propositioning any woman wearing a Porn-Star T-shirt with offers of work.

God

'Is there a God?' you may ask yourself as you look ruefully at the wreckage that is your 'life'. Of course there is. It can't *all* be your fault.

God's jokes

- Letting you know how much you loved someone just *after* you find out they're dating/marrying someone else.
- Thick luxuriant hair on your toes, none on your head (especially if you're female).
- Revealing 'the one' to be the bridesmaid/vicar on your wedding day.
- That yellow-headed throbbing nose pimple, the arrival of which coincides with a long-awaited date.
- That erection on the beach.
- Super-attractive to women – gay.
- Great hair day – no date!
- The obligatory attack of flatulence during oral sex.

Greens

An important food group providing essential vitamins and minerals. Sadly the mould growing on bread doesn't count.

Gym membership

If, when sunbathing on the beach, you're harpooned by a passing Japanese fishing boat, you may need to do a bit of body reshaping to improve your status in the Darwinian world of the singles market.

Gym etiquette

- Flirting. Although it's perfectly natural to eye people up in the gym, it is frowned upon to stare. Or dribble.
- Boxer shorts are a no-no when worn with loose-fitting shorts. They seriously increase the risk of what athletes refer to as ETS: Escaped Testicle Syndrome. This occurs when bench-pressing or stretching certain inner-thigh muscles. It's all too easy for the left or right hairy culprit to make an unannounced public appearance, looking rather like a baby ferret's head emerging from its set.
- Pace yourself on the cardiovascular machines. Being seen leaving the gym horizontally, with a nervous-looking paramedic holding electrodes to your heart and shouting: 'CLEAR', will not improve your pulling chances on your next visit.
- Don't wear make-up to the gym. Not only is it unnecessary, but no one wants to find an extra from an Ozzie Osbourne video sitting next to them in the sauna.

- Drinks holders on the treadmill machines are for water and isotonic fluids, not cans of lager.
- Ashtrays will not be provided under any circumstances.
- It is impolite to approach other members with: 'That's the wrong machine if you want to tighten up those saggy arse muscles.'
- Sweat – do wipe down any apparatus you use. This is good hygienic practice (not that that's any concern of yours) and if done deliberately and thoroughly will indicate to any women watching that you are good around the house and therefore worth taking home.
- While accidental farting is tolerated, for example when lifting heavy weights, 'following through' will result in a definite loss of gym membership.

H

Haircuts (*see also* Kudos)

A new hairstyle is a great way to re-build your confidence after a break-up. An added bonus if you go to one of the more upmarket salons is that you will also be given a sensual head massage (probably from some pimply assistant of the same gender, but if it's the nearest you're getting to coitus these days who cares?) when they wash your hair in that odd-shaped sink that looks like a urinal for a one-legged man.

> **TIP 1** If you are short of cash, you can pretend you've just had a haircut by sprinkling little bits of hair into your ears and over the bridge of your nose. For extra effect look at your reflection when passing shop windows and fiddle disgruntledly with your fringe muttering 'Butchers. I'm not going there again.'

> **TIP 2** Be careful when remarking disapprovingly to a date that her hair looks like she's just got out of bed. It probably took her hours of painstaking effort to achieve that look.

Hanging out with a couple (a.k.a. Adopt-a-singleton)

Although there can be benefits, do exercise caution when solving your lack of a social life by attaching yourself to a couple. You can quite easily become an unwitting part of a sophisticated money/labour saving scheme.

The 'ménage' and the 'à' of your 'trois' are sitting around having a gas:

HE: We found him feeding the ducks in the park and took him under our wing.

SHE: We don't know how we managed financially before we got him.

HE: Yes, he's a real boon. When the three of us go out, he pays a full half share in the restaurant, the taxi *and* when getting in a round.

SHE: It's great. He doesn't seem to mind getting the worst seat, the smallest room . . .

HE: . . . and of course it goes without saying that when we get a minicab, he's the one who has to sit in the front and talk to the driver.

SHE: I especially like the bag-minding service he provides when we go for a dance.

ENQUIRER: So what does he get out of it?

HE: Who knows? Isn't it fantastic?

SHE: (*to He*) Behave. (*To Enquirer*) We don't know what he gets from it. (*Whispering*) We think he doesn't like being on his own.

HE: Maybe he's just not very good at maths.
SHE: Shhh. Here he is now. (*To singleton*) Hi.
           Lovely to see you. You're just in time to
           make us all a cup of tea.

Holidays

As a single person it's very important that you take a
vacation, even if it means holidaying (shock, horror)
ALONE. How else are you going to strike up deep and
meaningful friendships with bored barmen, deck-chair
attendants and chip-munching seagulls, or stock up on
photos of strangers having a good time (in places that
you also visited but have no proof of being there). It's
also a great chance to practise the correct pronuncia-
tion in a foreign language of: 'Did you mind to keep an
eyeball on my sack while I am been to go for a swimming please?' (okay, you're a little rusty) and 'How do I
to get the adult movies on my TV? (*Underneath your
breath*) Yes I know it's only 8.00 a.m. Who are you, my
mother?'

> **TIP** If you want to save money on exotic, tropical holi-
> days why not simply sit fully clothed under your shower
> for two weeks and take a course of laxatives?

> **NOTE** If you get stung for the 'loser tax' (a.k.a. single
> person supplement) on your twin room, don't forget to
> set your alarm clock to go off in the middle of the night

so you can get out of one bed and into the other. After all, you've paid for it. (*See* S.A.D.)

How to spot a single man

If you want to avoid any painful errors (involving face-slapping and hairstyle-readjustment using fingernails and footwear) when dating, it's important to find out which men are attached, and which aren't. This also saves any unpleasantness later on in the relationship regarding which restaurants are 'safe' to visit and why you can't spend Christmas together.

Look out for the following signals, which are unfailing proof that the man in your sights is one hundred per cent available:

- When knocked down by a bus he is found to be wearing his swimming trunks in place of underwear.
- All his white T-shirts have turned a rather fetching hint of pink.
- When people ask who's going to the party, his name is always on the list, usually at the end preceded by 'Oh, and so and so, of course.'
- He can be found at those same parties in the kitchen, scoffing.
- The food in his beard doesn't seem to be bothering anyone.
- When attending a group picnic, his contribution comes in two forms – bottle or can.
- He's the one taking the communal photo.

- SHE: I know it's five o'clock in the morning, but do you know where we can get some alcohol and maybe a packet of Jammy Dodgers?

  HE: (*guiltily*) Yes I do.

- When friends look him up in their fifties, they discover he's dead.

How to spot a single woman

- Just wait a few seconds and she'll tell you.

  NOTE It is a sad fact that a lot of women waste their time complaining that there aren't any single men around. This is clearly untrue (do the maths), it's just that they don't know where to find them. This is easy. They're in the pub. Likewise the answer to 'where are all the single women?' is: they're in other single women's homes, sitting around complaining that there aren't any single men.

How to spot a single woman on holiday

Because women face many hassles when holidaying alone, some have taken to wearing bogus wedding rings to ward off unwanted attention. Therefore, to truly know if a woman is single or not, look for the tell-tale triangle of sunburn between the shoulder blades where she has found it impossible to apply sun cream by herself.

I

Icebreakers

Things not to say on a first date:
- Would you like to see my shrine to the others?
- I hope the food isn't too long, I've only got another hour left on this girdle.
- Do you think they'd warm a baby's bottle up for me in here?
- Thanks, my mum knitted it.
- Can you pick my napkin up for me, I don't want to burst my stitches.
- You looked quite sexy from behind.

Infidelity

If your partner has just admitted that they have been having an affair, tell a stranger. At least that way you weren't 'the last to know'.

Infra-red night goggles – *see* Advanced flirting

Intuition (female)

In the dating environment, it's important to follow your gut instincts.

HE: What do I drive? A Porsche of course.
SHE: So why are you wearing bicycle clips?
HE: (*looking down*) Ah.

Internet (*see also* Lonely hearts, Single person survival kit, Old school flames)

Who needs a partner when you've got the Internet?

> TIP One of the fun things about the Internet is you can use it to shop when you're drunk, although until you get the hang of it, you may find it disconcerting when three days after a late-night session a doner kebab arrives in the post.

Introductions

One of the thrills of dating is that it gives you the opportunity to meet so many new and wonderful people. Unfortunately some people (women) find it hard to say anything mean about their friends (What's the problem?

Isn't that what they're there for?) Even worse, they have a tendency to exaggerate the quality of their girlfriends' looks and personalities. Therefore when setting up a date based solely on female hearsay, it is important to read between the lines. The law of averages dictates that her single friends can't all be 'gorgeous'. To interpret her remarks correctly and avoid disappointment, use this helpful table:

She Says	You say
'Gorgeous and lovely'	'Sweet and dumpy'
'Totally mad'	'Totally drunk'
'Stunning'	'Someone who wears more make-up than Ronald McDonald'
'Shy but very sweet'	'Hello? Is there anybody in there?'
'Great fun and really down to earth'	'I'm sorry, your honour, she'd been drinking pints of wine all day and didn't realise she was giving a wedgie to a police officer'
'I can see what men see in her in a cheap sort of way'	'Cute!'

Of course, because men *never* want to pass on a potential shag to anyone else, they don't make introductions to friends.

Inviting someone back to your flat (*see also* Vacuuming)

Unless you live in a swanky penthouse with a live-in cleaner (who's not your mum) this might not be a good idea. All it does is give women the chance to indulge in a few of their favourite pastimes, namely nosing round other people's houses mentally rearranging the place as if they lived there, doing some sleuth-like checking for any signs of *female* habitation and of course poking fun at the shabby way you live.

If you must invite someone back, it's worth bearing in mind that people tend to form an impression – favourable or otherwise – from a subconscious calculation of all the available evidence. With this in mind, here is a simple points system to help you work out whether she will view your flat as a cosy love nest or a dodgy perv pad.

Binoculars, when there has been no declared interest in bird-watching	–10pts
Codpieces	–15pts
Plants:	
(alive)	+25pts
(dead but not pot pourri)	–10pts
(pot pourri)	–15pts
Specialist exotic magazines (*Hanky Spank-me, Chinchilla monthly, Readers' Goats*)	–15pts

Embarrassing health aids:

Truss	−5pts
(with pleasing detail)	+5pts
Special home sunlamp to combat rickets	−5pts
Penis-enlargement vacuum device	−15pts

Books on:

How to chat up women (except this one)	−5pts
How to give a great massage	+10pts
Salsa dancing	+10pts
Line dancing	−10pts
How to keep goats	−10pts

Any medicines relating to:

Bad breath	−5pts
Bottom itchiness	−5pts
Homicidal depression	−40pts

Any home-made self-pleasuring devices: −20pts to +15pts (depending on ingenuity of action)

Pictures of kittens or otters +10pts

Posters that focus too much on Gareth Gates or the male members of Liberty X −20pts

Any graphs or surveillance photographs detailing her recent movements −25pts

Any foodstuffs from the 'No frills' economy range −5pts

Children's drawings stuck on the fridge door:

from your own loins and previously declared	+5pts
from your own loins and previously undeclared	−50pts
Bailiffs' letters	−15pts
Luxury toilet paper	+30pts
Heating on	+50pts

Women looking to make a positive impression on any single men invited back might like to check their own homes against the following list:

Food in the fridge	+20pts
Beer in the fridge	+30pts

Photos showing you with exposed boobs:

on a designated beach	+10pts
at a party	+25pts
on the pitch during an FA cup final	+80pts
with an ex-boyfriend	−10 to −20pts
depending on handsomeness.	

Recycling crate containing:

Absinthe bottles	+10pts
Gin bottles	−10pts
Special Brew cans	−20pts
Cuddly toys	−2pts each
With names and introductions	−8pts each

Bathroom Cabinet products:

Moustache removing cream	−5pts
Feminine itching (whatever that means) medicines	−5pts
Condoms	+5 to −30pts
depending on quantity and exoticism (less is more)	

T-shirt with XXXL on the label	−5pts
Bra with XXXL on the label	+15pts
Wedding dress (used)	−10pts
Wedding dress (unused)	−75pts
Any of his underclothes stolen from his washing line	−30pts

Books:

How to live on a fiver	+10pts
The Karma Sutra	+15pts
if in the cookery section	−15pts
Women who love too much	−15pts
The Rules	−30pts
Football shirt signed by your favourite team	+50pts
Nightshirt signed by your favourite team	−50pts

J

Jealousy (*see also* The grass is greener)

As a single person you may have noticed that you have become an object of envy for your coupled-up, less 'free' friends. After all, who wouldn't want an *exciting* life of endless evenings spent watching the telly alone, tucking into a sumptuous banquet of cheap lager and skinheads on a raft (beans on toast), followed by *thrilling* nights trawling bars for someone with enough low self-esteem to be willing to perform a loveless act of copulation with a stranger, before finally admitting defeat and going home to the *freedom* of being able to tug yourself off into a coma and cry yourself to sleep?

> **TIP** If self-satisfied, married 'friends' are bugging you, feel free to use their misconceptions against them for a little light baiting.

FRIEND: (*smugly*) You know, I pity you.

YOU: (*stifling a yawn*) Oh yeah?

FRIEND: Why don't you settle down? You don't know what you're missing. You just can't beat a family (it's the law).

YOU:	Maybe.
FRIEND:	Have you any idea what's waiting for me at home?
YOU:	A bollocking?
FRIEND:	No.
YOU:	An atmosphere of icy ingratitude?
FRIEND:	No.
YOU:	Huge bills that will eventually consign you to an early grave?
FRIEND:	Hot pot. I love hot pot. What are you doing tonight?
YOU:	Well (*feigning humdrum tone*), me and a few mates are booked in to this new topless restaurant, and then later I'm going to a party with some off-duty lap dancers. (*Slyly*) You can come along if you want.
FRIEND:	I'll get my coat. (*Pause*) Any chance I can be back by half eight?

Just met

If you are single and enjoying a solitary meal in semi-darkness by the coats, occasionally sending up emergency flares in a vain attempt to attract the attention of passing waiters (*see also* **Eating alone**), a fun game to pass the time is spotting who is on a first date. Couples give themselves away if:

- She laughs at his 'tucking the napkin in the collar' joke.
- He shows an undue amount of care and attention in keeping her wine glass full to overflowing.

- They both read the menu from cover to cover while desperately thinking of something else that they can agree with each other about:

  HE: What do you think of breathing?

  SHE: I like it.

  HE: Me too. Isn't it great we like the same things?

- She *doesn't* crack the 'That's a big one (*snigger*), but I reckon I could manage it', giant pepper-grinder gag.
- He waits till she visits the bathroom before going ashen at the prices and locating the nearest exit.
- She *doesn't* come back from the bathroom excited because she's managed to jemmy open the giant loo roll holder and stuff the contents into her handbag.
- He does a very good job of stifling a yawn through that stuff about her cat's operation.
- She does a very good job of pretending not to be more interested in what the people on the adjacent table are talking about.
- There is no plate licking.

K

Karma

Buddhist term for spiritual process whereby the person who turned down your offer of marriage several years ago chokes to death on a lucky horseshoe wedding cake decoration.

Killjoy – *see* Chaperone

'Kiss of death'

The end of a relationship can often be traced back to one defining moment or decision.

- We don't need a telly, we've got each other.
- Can I have a look at your passport photo?
- I think we're grown up enough to share a bed without anything happening.
- . . . and this is one of me in leg-warmers.
- Would you like to meet my family?
- We're having a baby!

Knickers

It is common knowledge that most women operate a category system regarding their undergarments, the introduction to which depends on how well she knows you.

These tend to range from 'what's-the-point-pants' – the ones she wears in the first flush of love and which are so miniscule they make you think: 'what's the point?' – all the way to the bottom (ahem) end of the scale: 'period pants'. These are her worst-of-the-worst knickers worn, as the name implies, when a period is due. Formidable in size and construction, they can be detected by the VPL showing just under her armpits.

NOTE If, during a sexual clinch, you discover she is wearing a pair of period pants, don't be frightened. It merely indicates that she *really* meant it when she said she didn't expect all this to happen.

Kudos (*see also* Zealousness)

If you want to be successful with the opposite sex, you must show them love, respect and consideration, and if all goes well, over time they will give you as much in return. Or so the theory goes. However, if you are short of time and looking for a quick way to ingratiate yourself with a woman, you might like to try one of the following short-cuts (although I take no responsibility for the beatings you may receive if you get caught). One fast way to success is to slip things into the conversation like 'I think it's outrageous they still charge 5% VAT on sanitary products. They're NOT a luxury item' or 'I was watching *Sex and the City* on video the other night. That's *such* a good programme' and of course 'I really liked what you were saying earlier . . . (yes, I was listening)'.

Another quite effective trick is the 'new haircut' ruse. Every time you meet a woman, ask her if she's just had her hair cut. Nine times out of ten she won't have, but when you hit that one time – double gravy points for observation! Sadly, this doesn't work when asking about liposuction, boob jobs or whether you were right in thinking she'd just been done for shoplifting at Kwik-Save.

Women may care to shortcut their way into a man's affections with remarks like 'I don't know how you manage to shave *every* day. It must be so tiring' or 'I *love* your car. The (insert make of vehicle here) has always been one of my favourites. And you drive it like a musician' or 'I'm sorry for interrupting. What were *you* saying . . .?' Also any approving remarks about his 'pecs' (even if in truth it looks as though he may be lactating) or biceps, or simply remarking how much you like to take the tap end when sharing a bath, should pay handsome dividends later.

L

Lap-dancing

Do be careful when looking for thrills from this section of the entertainment industry. If you don't check the spelling, you may find yourself slipping fivers into the garters of some hairy, Finnish blokes doing a traditional jig celebrating the new snowfall around a stuffed reindeer (*see also* **Pole-dancing**).

'Lecher's neck'

Painful muscle strain which effects men during late spring when women start wearing those skimpy, see-through dresses.

Lesbians – how to spot them?

This is very easy. They're the ones that turn you down flat for a date – and frankly there's a lot of them about. (*See* **Speed dating**.)

Letting yourself go

If it's been a while since you last had a partner, you might have become a little *laissez faire* with your personal standards. But how far is too far?

- When people come into your house they wrinkle their nose and say 'I didn't know you kept hamsters. Has one of them died?'

- After a drunken night out you wake up to discover a chewed off female arm under your body.

- You've got Rentokil on speed dial, just next to The Samaritans and the local off-licence.

- You have decided it will be more convenient to live in just one room of the house, and have dragged your bed and TV into the kitchen. It also means you can be nearer your piles of locally collected refuse and soggy newspapers.

- Whenever you approach a perfume counter in a department store you sniff the air and say 'Mmm, I smell woman'.

- You've started wearing leather trousers, not as a fashion statement but because they are easier to keep clean – one wipe and that's your laundry done.

- When you approach friends you haven't seen for a long time, they say 'Sorry, we gave to the other bloke. Oh, it's you. You're looking . . . different.'

Lonely hearts ads – (*see also* Internet, Dating agencies, etc.)

These handy columns are a great way to meet the person of your dreams. However, you may notice that some people clog these important pages with patently overblown stuff about themselves, in the vain hope of ensnaring some poor, unfortunate soul into a loveless union. In my opinion, if you really want to stand out from the crowd, then the word here is HONESTY. Why not try:

Man seeks woman to share a few fun dates and then, as familiarity sets in, I'll take my foot off the gas and settle into a more regular routine of going to the pub with my mates, secretly watching porn when you've gone to bed, loud snoring and blowing off under the duvet. Interested?

Looking for Mr Right. Or will settle for an electric blanket with a driving licence.

Male, recently broke up with the love of my life, desperately seeking female to spend long, long nights listening to how amazing she was and what I'd do to get her back. No time-wasters.

Spinster, seen better days, with boobs you could plait, seeks gorgeous man (half toy-boy, half beast of the jungle) to whisk me off on fabulous, fornicating holidays. Or nearest offer.

I am: Male, 75, 5ft 1in, unattractive but loaded.
You are: None of the above.

Adulterer requires adult for adultery.

Deciphering the code:

WLTM	Would love to mess up/manipulate/moon (*delete as applicable)
GSOH	Great Set of Hooters, or Gonorreah, Syphilis or Herpes
LTR	Lying Toe-Rag
NTW	New to Watford
N/S	Not solvent
W/E	Wonky ears (nice of them to mention it)
ACA	A cute arse
GCH	Gas Central Heating . . . sorry, wrong advert

Love

If you've been through a few difficult relationships, you may have decided it's called *falling* in love because the process invariably leaves you on your knees and a step closer to the gutter.

Love bites

Classy teenage habit of creating a bruise by sucking hard on the skin (possibly with a vacuum cleaner), usually around the neck area (or wherever they can latch on to, they're not fussy). Despite efforts to keep these blemishes secret, mums usually know about them straightaway because there's a strong whiff of toothpaste following you around and you're watching TV in your balaclava.

Love Songs

As I've already mentioned, if you've been dumped recently and are feeling the strain, you may have noticed just how many love songs get played on the radio in a day. You may also be wondering if they are all secretly out to get you:

It's late afternoon. You are sat in the kitchen in your vest and pants. A tear-stained 'Dear John' letter lies crumpled on the table.

YOU: (*rising, to self*) Okay (*sniffle*) that's enough crying. It's time to pull yourself together. You've got to be strong. You may have lost her but you've still got your dignity. (*You notice a large dew drop hanging from your nose. You swiftly wipe it on to your pants.*) Remember now – this is the first day of the rest of your life (*deep sigh*). I'll put the radio on. Take my mind off things.

   Click

   'Don't Leave Me This Way' is playing.

YOU: Oh god.

   Click

   'And I Will Always Love You . . .'

YOU: Oh, bloody hell.

   Click

   'Who's Sorry Now?'

YOU: Urgh!

Click

'Only the lonely'

YOU: What the . . .?

Click

'Top Yourself You Loser'

YOU: Aarrrh!

Click – the radio is switched off.

Pause

YOU: Hang on, I don't remember that last one in the charts.

We hear the sound of a radio being flattened with a hammer.

YOU: (*to the beat*) Stop . . . messing . . . with . . . my . . . head.

Ten minutes later.

YOU: (*huge sigh*) That's better. Right, I'll put some Radiohead on, that'll cheer me up.

Love – the warning signs

Experts agree that 'love' is a very powerful emotional condition; in fact, some compare it to a serious mental disorder. In its early stages it can be very difficult to spot. However, if left untreated, more acute cases can develop into full blown relationships, the symptoms of which include: breathlessness, nausea, loss of appetite, mood swings, fatigue, localised swelling (hello!), mild ringing in the ears (sorry, wrong ailment) and pain when passing jewellery shops, all of which may become permanent.

TAKE ACTION NOW IF:

Men:

- You notice you are secretly holding a fart in for three hours when in her company.
- You feel no embarrassment when she sits on your knee in the pub.
- You remember her birthday or at least that she has one.
- Your friends have a vague awareness of her existence.
- You don't reach for your passport when she misses her period.
- You have a worrying, gormless smile fixed on your face, similar to the expression a dog has when it sticks its head out of the car window.

Women:

- You notice you are secretly holding a fart in for three years in his company.
- You feel no embarrassment when he murders 'Angels' on Karaoke night.
- You begin feeding him *before* the cat.
- Your friends know the time and date of his appendix operation in 1987, and the name of the surgeon.
- You notice on shopping trips that trying on clothes takes twice as long as usual, as you ponder what *he* would think of you in them.

- You have a worrying loss of interest in both confectionery and your own identity.

If symptoms persist seek advice from *The A-Z of Living Together.*

Love vs. lust

With love, the bruises are on the inside.

M

Mad girlfriends (*see also* Psycho boyfriends)

Commiserations if you are unlucky enough to have fallen for someone who thinks the correct thing to say to a gang of passing skinheads is: 'Who are *you* looking at? If you don't piss off, my boyfriend will beat the lot of you up, won't you? (*Turning to you*) What are you doing on your knees?'

Making an effort

Some women complain that men don't make an effort when taking them out. The simple truth is: Is he dressed? Yes? Then he's made an effort.

Marriage

Don't worry about being single and not getting any offers of marriage. Remember, swans mate for life and look how bad tempered they are.

Maturity

That growing sense of worldliness which manifests itself as your being able to offer physical comfort to a female friend without groping.

Mistakes (sexual)

We all make mistakes with sex. It's easily done as we shove our tongue into a sour-tasting, chalky armpit, or have to be extracted from our vehicle alongside our partner, pained and bandy-legged, having suffered a double hand-brake and gear stick penetration. It's all part of the fun of discovery and causes no harm, except for maybe some mild psychological scarring to the AA man. Other common intimacy errors we make include:

Sex in the vertical (standing) position
Before attempting this feat, it is essential you get an accurate weight measurement from your partner (preferably in writing from her GP). Guessing, or worse, *taking her word for it*, can lead to a lifetime of expensive physiotherapy treatments.

You are both enjoying a moment in the missionary position. Keen to let her know just what a 'player' she is dealing with, you have an idea.

YOU: Okay sweetheart (*showing her who's boss*) how about I just pick you up and . . . (*You go to lift her to the position where her legs are wrapped around your waist. You've seen it on late-night TV, it looks easy. It's not.*) Crikey, you're heavier than you look aren't you? (*Your knees begin to buckle*)

SHE: (*embarrassed*) Put me down then. (*She begins to struggle. This doesn't help.*)

YOU: Eight stone, you say? I think not.

SHE: (*shouting*) Put me down, NOW.

YOU: Okay. (*Reddening in the face*) I will. (*You try to lower her gently back on to the bed. She's not convinced it's going to be a smooth landing.*) Could you let go of my hair, love? Please let go. Just a bit more. You're hurting me now. I won't drop you, I promise. You've got hold of my sideburns. . . (*You find yourself locked at the mid point where your spinal column is taking all her weight – it is the lifting position seen on factory safety posters with a large red cross through it. There is a loud cracking noise*) Oh god, my back! (*Crumbling, you both fall on to the bed where she receives an accidental head butt from you just to add to the joy of the moment.*)

SHE: (*angry for being outed by you as 'bulky'*) You sod. I didn't want to be picked up. (*She rubs her head*)

YOU: (*oblivious, rolling and groaning*) Oh, my back. (*You look down at your crotch. It doesn't look good either – although to be honest it never did*) Look at that. (*She goes to prod it.*) Don't! It really hurts. It's not designed to point to the floor in its 'proud' state you know. I think it's broken. You've broken it . . .(*You begin to whimper.*)

SHE: Oh, shut up, you baby. It was like that when you gave it to me. It's your fault anyway. With your gymnastics . . .

YOU: (*sniffling*) I can't talk right now. I'm in a lot of pain.

SHE: Is there anything I can get you?

YOU: Yes, some ice and a couple of lolly sticks for a splint please.

SHE: Anything else?

YOU: Erm, I'd quite like a car. (*See **The A–Z of Living Together**.*)

Sex on a heavy-weave (sea-grass) carpet

A foolhardy and painful activity that will leave you with knees looking like Ryvitas and your partner with an arse like a waffle. (*See also **Passion**.*)

Having a finger inserted into the wrong place (i.e. bottom)

The important thing here is to ASK FIRST. When it comes from nowhere, understandably, it's a shock to the system:

YOU: (*recoiling*) What the bloody hell was that? (*You jump out of bed in a panic and search the room*) Who's there? Who's there? Come out from there, wherever you are. (*To your partner*) Did you see anyone? I think I've just been anally trespassed.

SHE: (*embarrassed*) It was me.

YOU: (*shocked*) You? What the hell are you playing at? I might need counselling now.

SHE: I thought you might like it.

YOU: (*recovering your composure*) Well, you might want to give me a bit of warning next time instead of wham, bam here comes Harry the hand.

SHE: Stop being so melodramatic. It was barely a fingertip.

YOU: Barely a tip? I could feel your watch.

SHE: Now you're being silly.

YOU: I'm not. Honestly, for a moment I felt like Sooty.

SHE: (*hurt*) Well don't worry, I won't be doing it again. (*And adding ominously*) Or anything else for that matter.

YOU: (*noting the threat*) Oh, come on, love. I'm sorry. (*In best little boy's voice*) You can do whatever you like, you know that. Treat me like a Dutch dyke if you want. Just do me a favour next time – ask before you try something European, okay?

Multi-tasking

An impressive (female) ability to do many things at once. Indeed, to see a woman manage to hold a conversation with you, apply lipstick in the rear-view mirror *and* crash the car all at the same time is a never-to-be-forgotten experience. However, under certain conditions men have been known to achieve a similar level of skill and dexterity: drunkenly walking home, eating a burger, having a pee and texting 'Sorry 4 bng L8 just lvng wrk now xox' all at the same time.

N

Name-calling

There are times when maturity and reasonableness must take a back seat. For instance: finding yourself in possession of a handful of ice-cubes and spotting a particularly inviting bum cleavage at a party. Or, indeed, when you get to hear about your ex's 'lovely' new partner.

Big and clever things to call her new bloke (behind his back of course):

- That Streak Of Piss (good for spitting out bitterly between hacking sobs with your head buried into a friend's supportive shoulder).
- Mr Sloppy Seconds (which doesn't bear thinking about).
- 'Him' (to the point).
- Knobhead (always a favourite).
- Mr Too-Good-To-Be-True-If-You-Ask-Me (no one does).
- The Home-Wrecker (good for female sympathy).
- Plonker (works in mixed company).

Big and clever things to call his new girlfriend
- 'Her'
- The Witch
- The Bimbo
- Miss Bad Dye Job
- The Frump
- Good Luck To Her

TIP When you're feeling low and looking for a suitable word to describe the person who has just trampled on your hopes and dreams, you might be wondering: What is the difference between the colloquial terms 'slag' and 'bitch'? The received wisdom on this is that a slag is someone who sleeps with everyone, and a bitch is someone who sleeps with everyone except you.

NOTE Sadly, the author is not aware of any (printable) male equivalents to the above.

Neediness

Both men and women are rightly fearful of this kind of behaviour, so feel free to disguise it as very strong love.

Nirvana

If this is the word that springs to mind when *you* close your eyes and *they* shut their gob, you may need to think about where this particular relationship is going.

No

The correct answer to:

- Have you ever slept with . . .? (Don't even wait for the rest of this question, the answer is No. Period.)
- Would you get back with your ex if . . .? (See above.)
- Can I have your last Rolo? (No one likes a creep.)
- Is this just sex for you?
- Have you given my pet name to anyone else?
- Do you know who shaved my eyebrow off?
- I'll bet you're completely different when you're out with your mates, aren't you?
- Did you really fancy my friend?
- Was it you who sent me that Valentine's card containing a pair of photocopied buttocks?
- Was that you I saw coming out of the genito-urinary clinic last week?
- Would you like a lift? I know a shortcut down some deserted country lanes.

Non-acceptance (that it's over)

Sometimes it's hard to say what we really mean to the person we loved and who cruelly dumped us. Sometimes it's even harder to accept that there's no possible chance of reconciliation. (*See also* **Winning him/her back.**)

It's 3.00 a.m. You are in your flat. The receiver is at your ear. She finally answers.

YOU: (*before she has a chance to speak*) Hi, it's me.

SHE: (*with a weary sigh*) Oh, hi. I just got in.

YOU: (*to self: where have you been till now? No, don't tell me – I'll die*) That's nice.

SHE: Have you been phoning long?

YOU: (*Of course I've been phoning long. I've been hitting redial for the past seven hours, I've got a swollen finger and the receiver's practically melting in my hand*) No. This is the first time. Must be telepathic (*and therefore made for each other*). (*Pause.*) Hello?

SHE: Was there something specific you phoned for? I'm very tired.

YOU: (*Ouch! So cold. This is going to be harder than I thought.*) There's some post here for you. (*It's only a pizza delivery leaflet, but please come round, I would love to see you.*)

SHE: Oh, okay. I'll come over and get it. (*Yippee*) But, it'll have to be next week now. (*Boo hoo.*)

YOU: (*hurt and curt*) I'd rather you didn't. (*Don't listen to me. Yes, please, I'd love you to come round now, bring some overnight clothes, stay the night and tell me it's all been a terrible mistake. I really miss you.*)

SHE: If that's what you want.

YOU: (*No, it's not. And you agreed to that much too quickly!*) (*Then, hesitant*) It is. (*Don't listen to me – I'm the one who's been dumped. I haven't got any power anymore. Being crappy is the only card I've got left. Can't you see through this charade?*)

SHE: Okay, I'll get a friend to collect it.

YOU: (*A boyfriend? You've got a new boyfriend? Already?*
        Somebody kill me.) Fine. I'll be in between 7:00
        and 7:02. (*Take that, cow.*)

Long pause

SHE: So, how are you?

YOU: (*How long have you got?*) How do you think I am?
        (*I'm enjoying this. Now say: 'I think you're upset*
        because I've been a heartless bitch, but it doesn't matter
        because I'm coming back to you', or words to that effect.)

SHE: I don't know.

YOU: (*Close enough.*) (*Blurting*) Do you think there's any
        chance we might get back together?

SHE: (*with another weary sigh*) I don't think there's any
        chance of that happening.

YOU: (*Don't* think, *eh? I sense uncertainty.*) I love you.

SHE: (*knowing where this is going*) Thank you. Look,
        I've got to go.

YOU: (*I understand. Obviously the feelings you have for me*
        are too strong – it's all getting a bit emotional.) I'll
        drop your mail off then, should I? (*It's only a forty*
        mile round trip completely out of my way. It's no
        problem. I can be there in twenty minutes. It'll be like
        old times.)

SHE: I'd rather you didn't. Please, this is very hard for
        me, but I don't think you should call again.

YOU: (*Ah, she's heartbroken, poor girl*) Okay, if that's what
        you want. (*I think we both know it isn't.*)

SHE: Yes, it is. I'm sorry. Goodbye.

She hangs up.

YOU: I think that went very well. A few more calls like
that and she'll be putty in my hands.

O

Off limits

If you wish to remain on the right side of a new (female) partner, it's important to remember that some things are sacrosanct. These include her secret stash of slimming bars ('they're not biscuits'), her dreams ('will you stop laughing? I was very frightened. I thought I was going to be stuck in green blancmange forever') and those free perfume/moisturiser samples attached to the pages of her magazines. If she comes home to find you wearing half a green-mud face-pack, with one arm covered in fake tan and reeking of Anaïs Anaïs, she might not find it as funny as you think.

Likewise, there are some things men don't like other people messing with either: his goldfish (you've fed him how many times?); his toolbox (can somebody explain why there's marmalade on my chisels?); the position of his rear view mirror (*see* **Multi-tasking**) and especially that Kinda Egg Surprise toy he was really looking forward to putting together with a nice cup of tea.

Office romances

A highly efficient way to inform *all* your work colleagues of any deeply personal and extremely embarrassing sexual peccadilloes you may have. (*See also* **Manhood dimensions**, **Embarrassing underwear**, **Thomas the Tank Engine duvet covers**, etc.)

> **NOTE** The same effect can also be achieved by hitting the wrong button on your e-mail program.

Old school flames

A great way to find a new partner these days is to simply dig up an old one from one of the many school reunion sites on the Internet. However, if your synopsis of what you've been up to since leaving school reads:

After a couple of nervous breakdowns, three divorces and a spell in prison, I can now be found sleeping rough in Rhyl. I'm the one who likes to dance a jig and wave at traffic in the town centre and who smells of Camembert cheese. How's everyone else doing?

you might want to think of a different approach (or tell a few lies).

On the rebound (*see also* Finding yourself, Revenge shags, etc.)

Excellent excuse for sleeping with utterly unsuitable individuals.

On your own

Things that are better done ALONE
- Sleeping in a very hot room.
- Planning a route.
- Eating a large bar of expensive Swiss chocolate.
- Watching a Jenny Agutter movie (grrrr!)
- Receiving praise or a cash reward.
- Losing your dignity.
- Counting your money (especially if you have more than you should).
- Panicking.
- Riding a Shetland pony.
- Threading a needle.
- Playing pass the parcel.
- Recognising yourself on *Crimewatch*.

You see, single life can have direction and meaning.

One-night stands (*see also* Christmas parties)

An empty, hollow, drunken (am I getting warm?) sexual experience that leaves you feeling guilt-ridden, cheap and strangely gluey as you wake up at 6.00 a.m. with breath a cat would be ashamed of and try to find your way out of the sheltered accommodation block. Followed by the 'walk of shame' – that embarrassing journey from the scene of your sleazy night-time mischief to your own pit of squalor, with your underwear on back to front, only one sock on, smelling of stale cigarettes and Femfresh and ultimately being the only person in the early morning bus queue in fancy dress.

> **TIP 1** If you want to avoid the toe-curling awkwardness of facing your one night stand the following morning, you should always make sure you secure an invitation to their flat rather than bringing them home (*see also* **Invitations**). That way you don't have to surreptitiously coerce them into leaving by telling little white lies about your mum (who has a weak heart) coming round soon, your awful boss who makes you work Sundays (and how you really must finish writing that sermon) or being a member of the armed forces who has suddenly been called away to . . . *insert name of un-checkable faraway place here*.

TIP 2 If you are lying guiltily in bed after a particularly late, midweek night out, and the sound of the dawn chorus is stopping you from getting to sleep, it might help to imagine the birds have been out boozing all night too and are on their way home from bars and clubs; hence the raucous singing.

Orgasms

If you have to fake one (for example when you lose control too quickly in the company of a new partner, unwisely labour on as if by pretending it didn't happen you can fool your cerebral cortex, and then realise you are now losing your erection . . . oh. Just me again?), remember: modern women are not so easily fooled. For complete authenticity, when visiting the bathroom afterwards, don't forget to spray pee over the toilet seat and surrounding areas to imitate the dodgy targeting ability of post-orgasmic male plumbing.

P

Parties

Unless you want to remain unattached for the rest of your life, do follow these simple guidelines:

The Don'ts and Really Don'ts of parties:

- Don't arrive too early. It's considered bad manners to be found lurking on your host's doorstep when he gets home from work, guzzling your fourth can of strong lager and chatting up his elderly next-door neighbour.
- Don't forget to use the toilet before leaving home. It will do your image no good if you come out the bathroom and have to say to a long queue of groovy party people: 'I'd leave it a few minutes in there if I was you'.
- Don't find yourself alone in the lounge reading the host's CD covers. Unless you are the host, and the party's long finished.
- Don't be the first and only person on the dance floor, unless you're someone's fearsome auntie and Abba's 'Dancing Queen' has just come on, in which case it's understood you just can't help yourself.

- Don't get drunk and pass out in anyone's vomit other than your own.
- Don't be the one stupid enough to ask everyone at 2.00 a.m.: 'Who'd like a nice cup of tea?' (This has nothing to do with meeting people, it's just common sense.)
- Don't call any mystery phone numbers found in your wallet the next day and open the conversation with: 'Hi, remember me? Oh come on, you must. I was the one who made the smell in the loo everyone was talking about.'

'Pash rash' (*see also* XXXs)

Giveaway facial redness, caused by long bouts of snogging, which suggests there may be more to that mysterious blonde with the big feet and huge Adam's apple than you first thought. Still, what a kisser! (*See also* **Dogs**)

Passion

That elusive emotion we all look for in a relationship, which somehow makes us temporarily oblivious to the pain caused by carpet burns to bums, knees and chins. (*See also* **Sex on sea-grass carpeting**)

Pet names

Please do the rest of us a favour and keep these strictly for the bedroom. Thanks babycakes.

Pettiness

During a break up, it is possible (and admittedly quite a lot of fun) to become a little grudging in your behaviour.

Are you both being too petty?
- You send her twenty-six playing cards and half a joker.
- She posts back a single hair found in the bathroom with an accompanying note saying: This is YOURS, I believe.
- You return her prized cacti collection, make-up (lids removed) and bed linen all in the same bin liner.
- She instructs her solicitors to pursue you through the courts for the retrieval of the consonants from the Scrabble set.
- You agree she can borrow the car, but not the keys.
- She allows you access to the dog on the strict proviso that you don't stroke it or look it directly in the eyes.
- You refuse to sign any divorce papers for several years citing a 'leaky pen'.
- She takes out a full-page advert in the local paper declaring that you are not the father of the children on the grounds that you are clinically impotent.
- In a fit of rage you take her elderly parents hostage in their bungalow.

- She is summoned from work by the police to talk you out of your promise to 'start spilling claret soon'.
- You open the door to hear her out, only to be rushed by the Police Tactical Support Squad and immediately 'taken out' with a shot through the temple, the exiting bullet sadly catching your ex in the heart killing her instantly.

So do try to be civil to each other.

Pheromones

It's a scientific fact that smell can be a good indication of compatibility. However, although sweat can be a powerful aphrodisiac, this doesn't necessarily mean *all* types of sweat. Retrieving the stuff from the crack of your bottom after a long bike ride in lycra shorts and dabbing it behind your ears might not get you the results you're looking for in the nightclub.

Phoning back

For some reason, the length of time it takes you to call after the first date is of huge significance. The trouble is, you can't win. If you don't call for a week, this is frowned upon. Yet if you phone immediately and then follow it up every five minutes throughout the night (maybe with a few dozen text messages and a couple of bomb scares thrown in for good measure), they don't like that either.

Platonic relationships

Those friendships which we all know involve at least one person living a lie.

'Plenty more fish in the sea'

Oh yeah? Haven't they heard about over-fishing?

Powdered milk (in your tea)

Along with a pungent, lingering smell of joss sticks and bone idleness and a vague recollection of discussing globalisation till you ran out of Rich Tea biscuits and Rizlas, this is a good indication that the person who pulled you last night was a student.

Power (*see also* What do men want?)

It is a well-known fact that women find power and status irresistible (*see* **David Mellor, Bernie Ecclestone, That bloke who was married to Mariah Carey**). So it follows that to improve your chances with women you should look for ways to attain these qualities.

> **TIP** If you want to acquire a superior attitude instantly, why not consider becoming a vegetarian or a cyclist for the afternoon?

WARNING Although technically a position of 'power', being the person who controls the music during a game of pass-the-parcel at a children's party does not necessarily confer woman-pulling status upon you. Nor will it help your cause if you are seen punching the air and saying: 'Did you see that? I didn't let the little chubby one with glasses get a single go at unwrapping it and now he's gone home crying. Wow. I *love* this game.'

Psycho boyfriends (*see also* Mad girlfriends)

Bad luck if you've fallen head over heels for someone who wants to punch the lights out of the man he caught you smiling at, even after you've explained he's your Dad.

Pretend girlfriend/boyfriend

If you are having difficulty procuring a partner, don't be disheartened. With a little bit of imagination it is quite easy to simply *pretend* you have a girlfriend or boyfriend.

For women this can be achieved by:
● Not listening to yourself.
● Giving yourself a running commentary in the car on how badly everyone else is driving.
● Leaving the fridge door open for no reason whatsoever.

- Buying yourself cheap and scratchy underwear that was clearly bought for a slut half your size.
- Neglecting all your friends.
- Telling yourself that lifting your legs up to let the vacuum cleaner pass underneath is doing half of the housework.
- Buying coloured loo roll that doesn't match the bath-room.
- Undermining your own confidence.
- Giving yourself and others Christmas and birthday presents wrapped in old newspaper held in place by band-aids.
- Reckoning that all remote control problems can be fixed simply by taking out the batteries, giving them a quick rub whilst simultaneously breathing on them, putting them back in, then tapping the device several times on your thigh. Hey presto - fixed.
- Getting in the way of yourself when looking in the mirror.
- Strapping a couple of dead rodents to the radiator for that comforting 'blokey' smell.
- *Reader to add own here . . .*
- *Reader to add own here . . .*

For men why not:
- Keep asking yourself what you're thinking.
- Tell yourself you're going to a wedding only two hours before it's due to start – and then complain to yourself all the way there that you never listen to anything you say.

- Drive yourself mad by singing loudly out of tune while guessing half the words to every song in the Top 40.
- Force yourself to stay awake for several hours after a bout of self abuse, talking about 'us'.
- Spend Saturday afternoons looking at thirty-seven different yellow tops and then say you can't afford one anyway.
- Serve up dinner right on kick off.
- Constantly tell yourself to slow down in an annoying voice when driving.
- Tell all your pals' girlfriends your embarrassing habits and then laugh it off later as 'just a bit of fun'.
- Wash your towels.
- Stop the conversation abruptly, regardless of how serious, whenever a favourite tune comes on the radio and say 'Oh, I love this song.'
- Leave large clumps of hair in the bath plug hole so it eventually begins to look like Leo Sayer.
- *Reader to add own here . . .*
- *Reader to add own here . . .*

Pride

One of the seven deadly sins so give it up. It gets in the way of all the fun.

Pulling (on your own)

Try to avoid going out alone to meet the opposite sex. For some reason women are rarely attracted to the 'creepy loner' look and there are quite a few men who find the 'Nora no-mates'-type quite disturbing too (until the end of the evening when the 'slowies' come on of course).

Q

Qualms

Those annoying little guilt pangs you get during a fit of loneliness and self-loathing, when you comfort yourself by eating all the dog's chocolate treats.

Quandaries

Being single presents you with some interesting little conundrums, such as:

- Should I have a piece of lightly grilled fish and a jog in the park or another packet of Jammy Dodgers and think about doing myself in?
- Should I be turned down by a luscious blonde or a busty brunette tonight?
- What flavour of crisps/ice cream should I have for my Sunday dinner this week?
- Should I buy myself a miner's helmet or replace some of the blown light bulbs in the flat?
- Hmm. I want to move on from this failed relationship, but am enjoying all the attention and extra sympathy I

am getting from moping around a lot and whining like an infant. What to do?

- Which seat should I take on public transport? The one next to the deranged nutter or the one next to the morbidly obese chatterbox?
- *Razzle* or *Hustler*?

Quids in

Popular expression used to describe your financial state now you're single and not being bled dry by another human being for bus fares, petrol, magazines, top-up phonecards and polka dot shoes because 'they were in the sale'. Now you are free to spend it on some decent therapy (*see* **Trips to Amsterdam**).

R

Red-wine lips

Disturbing purple tinge affecting the lips and gums that indicates the sufferer has a blood–alcohol level high enough to let you know a) how much she loves you b) how much she hates you c) why those bastards at work/her mother don't give her the respect she deserves and d) that a request for a bucket to be brought up to bed will follow very shortly. (*See also* **What do women need from men?**)

Reconciliation

Bad reasons for getting back together
- You couldn't be bothered taking the sidecar off your motorbike.
- She needed some new razors.
- You'd just trained her up to make a decent cup of tea.
- She needed to get something down from a high shelf.
- The bathroom cabinet felt empty without her.
- She worked out you were marginally cheaper to run than an electric blanket.

- You couldn't find anyone else to fit the dent she left in the mattress.
- You're better than nothing (just).

Relaxing

Why not do what a lot of recently bulleted individuals do and lie awake in the dead of night, staring at the ceiling, and have a long, hard think about everything that's wrong with your life. Ah, bliss.

Revenge shag (*see also* Emergency shag, On the rebound, etc.)

A dubious action performed by a rejected partner, usually with a complete stranger. The aim is not sexual gratification but a desire to cause hurt – unless you're the lucky stranger that is, in which case, let them feel your pain!

SHE: You know this means nothing to me, don't you?
HE: Yes I do and that's not a problem. How do you want me?

Rugs (sheepskin)

If you are serious about creating the right mood for seduction then you should think about making a few quality investments. (*See also* **Satin sheets**, **Velvet handcuffs**, **Sade CDs**, **Velcro underpants**, etc.) Laid out in front of a roaring open fire, a luxurious rug can't be beaten for style and sophistication. If, however, this is beyond your means, I've found it can work just as well to lay your Snorkel parka out in front of a three-bar electric fire, get her to perch on the fur bit of the hood and use her imagination.

S

S.A.D.

(Single And Discriminated *or* 'Why my life is so much harder than everyone else's'.)

Feel free to read this statement out loud to yourself each morning. Once you've got it off your chest you can forget about all the cruel injustices you face in this solo-phobic world and get on with complaining about something useful like why you can't get chocolate on the NHS.

'Being single is really difficult because you can't take up any two-for-one offers and when you go on holiday there's no one to hold your towel when you're getting changed and you have to take your bags everywhere because you haven't got anyone to mind them while you go for a pee and you put on weight because all ready-meals are for two and so you end up eating both portions which if that isn't a vicious circle I don't know what is and it's difficult to keep appointments with tradesmen because there isn't someone to stay put if you need to go somewhere urgently and you have to make *all* the decisions which is really tiring especially if you're not very confident and you can't play on the see-saw and have you ever tried putting cuff-links in? forget it and they won't let you order the assorted starters in a Chinese restaurant and everyone knows they're the best bit or any of those set banquets and you don't get invited to wife-swapping parties or to dinner parties for that matter because you're not in with the 'couple mafia' or worse they patronise you and treat you like their little pet and say things like 'We'll give you a lift, you don't mind squeezing in the back with the child seat do you?' well actually yes I do and when you share a taxi with a couple and it comes to paying they count themselves as 'one' – how does that work? and they get the comfy back seat as if it's their right and if you're in a round they count themselves as 'one' again the tight bastards and they think you don't notice well we bloody do notice and solitaire is nowhere near as much fun as tennis and snogging and it's hard work carrying all the shopping in on your own and there's no one to back you up in an argument or tell you when you've cooked the best spaghetti bolognese ever and you don't feel right walking in the park on your own especially if you're wearing your new balaclava and if you go to a wedding they make you feel like you're a nuisance and they don't know what to do with you so they put you next to someone's granny for dinner or worse on the kids' table and you spend all the time declining offers to swap your jelly for their peas and what if I fell down the stairs and died eh? Who'd be there to find me? The bloody bailiffs probably chancing on my desiccated body half-eaten by snails when they kick my door down looking to seize my goods and chattels to cover the non-payment of the bill for the new stair carpet which I said wasn't fitted properly anyway but they couldn't fix it because I didn't have anyone to stay in for them and all this for 25 per cent discount on my fucking council tax? (*Deep breath*) There, I feel better already.'

Sade (*pronounced* Shar-day)

Owning at least one of this artist's CDs is a must for any serious dater, offering the perfect inoffensive musical accompaniment (*see also* **The Lighthouse Family, Sting, Lionel Ritchie**) to making the first move on your date. Unless, that is, you make the fatal error of saying 'Slip your coat off babe. I'll just put some 'Say-die' on,' in which case you might as well re-cork the 'Ree-O-ja', call her a cab, grab a good book and pop your Superman pyjamas on.

Seven stages of a relationship

If, as a single person, you can't bear to know what you are missing out on domestically, please skip the next page . . .

Stage 1
Holding Hands

Stage 2
Pet Names

Stage 3
Flatulent Familiarity

Stage 4
B&Q

Stage 5
Matching Tracksuits

Stage 6
Twin Beds

Stage 7
Death

Sex objects

Most men struggle to understand why women don't like being thought of as sex objects.

SHE: (*angrily*) You men are all the same. All you want to do is treat women as sex objects. How would *you* like it if every girl you met just wanted to have sex with you?

YOU: I'm not even going to answer that question.

Shopping (in supermarkets)

I know that shopping is boring. I know that you'd prefer to go shopping only when they've built a trolley big enough for *you* to sit in. I know that shopping can be confusing when the shops don't sell what they're supposed to sell; you can't get a curry in Currys, you can't buy boots in Boots and Superdrug is a huge disappointment. But remember – research has shown that supermarkets are hotbeds of hidden flirting and sexual intrigue. If you want to be a player in the singles scene you will have to get in there and start exchanging meaningful glances over the pickled gherkins and the crusty baps.

TIP You can learn a lot about someone from the contents of their shopping basket (e.g. avoid people whose shopping consists solely of cream cakes, Ex-lax and breath mints, or bottles of gin, tissues and chocolate dog treats, or indeed baby oil and bananas. Hrrrrrgh!). So why not use the information you've gleaned as part of your chat-up routine? When you spot someone you fancy, go up to them, point at an item they intend to buy and make polite conversation about it. Simple. Although you may need to be a little more imaginative than 'Hey, loo roll. So, you go to the toilet? Me too. What a lovely coincidence' or 'Head and Shoulders? I didn't know you had a scabby, flaking scalp' or 'Nice buns – and I don't mean your arse'.

Single person's survival kit

As a single person, you will sometimes have different needs and requirements from someone in a couple. This shouldn't be too much of a problem. All you need to do is get together a few essential items to carry with you at all times:

- A book – to give you something to pretend to do when waiting for dates, dining alone or to hide behind when you spot your ex having more fun than you (unless the book is called *How to stop being a loser*).
- Sunglasses – to hide bloodshot eyes, look mysterious, ogle with impunity and, if you live in Britain, give off an air of hopeless optimism.
- Rope and grappling hook – for when you've forgotten to replace the loo roll and the spare is under the kitchen sink.
- Your own candle (*see* **Eating Alone**).
- Mobile phone – so that you can be forgotten and ignored *wherever* you go.

- A fertile imagination – or failing that a credit card and Internet connection.

Sisters

You may think that having sisters will give you a deeper understanding of women. It doesn't. This is because sisters are not women. They are a strange third sex. Ask yourself this – would you go out with a woman if, every time you did something wrong, she pinned you to the ground and let a length of spittle dribble slowly towards your face before sucking it back up again, until you apologised to her satisfaction? No, I didn't think so.

Sleeping alone

If you have recently split with a live-in lover you may be wondering why you are still sleeping six inches from the edge of the mattress. This is called Lack Of Closure. Other examples include still paying double for everything in restaurants, ducking after emitting a loud and lengthy burp, denying you ate all the biscuits and waking up in a cold sweat shouting: 'Damn you, you've ruined my life.'

Sod's law (*see also* God's jokes)

The frustrating phenomenon which states that if something can go wrong, it will. For example: when the food arrives the moment you light a cigarette (which is annoying, especially when it happens in your own house – why do you do that?). Or, when you accidentally drop a partner while attempting to re-enact a scene from *Last Tango in Paris*, she always lands butter-side down.

TIP Why not use sod's law to your advantage? When going out for the evening, try dressing in your worst clothes – maybe don a pair of pyjama bottoms with an old Afghan coat. Underneath, wear a flared, holey T-shirt and those attractive pink nylon Y-fronts that you once used as a duster and that now have an unfortunate stain up the back. Or simply go for the classic socks and sandals look. Suitably attired, you'll be guaranteed to meet an endless stream of fit, unattached, sexy women.

Women: how about going out on the town wearing not a scrap of make-up, in saggy-arsed leggings that are laddered around the crotch, and with a nice mop of greasy 'Don King'-style hair piled up on your head. Sporting American tan tights with hairy legs is always a winner too. Better still, time your night out to coincide with a visit to the dentist that results in your having a couple of wisdom teeth removed – you'll be amazed at how many funny, clever, George Clooney look-alikes you'll bump into in one night.

Speed dating

YOU: Hi.

SHE: Piss off.

YOU: Thank you for your time.

Spontaneity

A great way to add 'zing' (whatever that is) to your sex life is to now and again let your carnal urges take over in a frenzy of mutual desire, without giving a second thought to the constraints of modern manners or your worrying lack of basic suppleness. However, before engaging in such spontaneous acts, do make sure:

- You are not wearing thigh-length lace-up boots under drainpipe trousers.
- You didn't go for the tight-fitting jumper and dangly earrings look today.
- You are not wearing your Christmas underpants.
- You haven't started the proceedings too close to the cat litter tray.
- You don't have small children loose in the house.
- The doors are locked.
- The curtains are drawn.
- Condoms are handy.
- The handbrake is on.
- The parking meter is paid.
- The phone is unplugged.
- The dog is out of the room (very important).

- The cat doesn't feel sick.
- You haven't ordered anything that needs to be signed for.
- You've got household insurance.
- The neighbours aren't planning to return anything.
- Your ears are clean.
- Your knees can take it.
- You've got a really strong back.

Or you could wait till bedtime – like normal people.

Sunday blues (*see also* Spring blues, Summer blues, Weekend-break blues)

The feeling you get, as a single person, when you're stuck behind your thirty-seventh smooching, dawdling, canoodling, hand-holding couple in IKEA, and you want to strangle them with something from the stylish yet functional Smöft bedroom lamp range.

Sunday cheer

The feeling you get when you see the same couple pulled up in a lay-by, shouting and finger-pointing an inch from each other's face about whose job it was to check the knots, just after you've swerved to avoid hitting a comfy yet knackered Klęft sofa bed sitting in the middle of three lanes of speeding traffic.

T

Talking dirty

It's a strange fact but true that women are much better at talking dirty than men. That is why there are far more adverts in the back of magazines that feature scantily clad women offering phone sex than glad-eyed men in their pants promising to give your ears an aural pleasuring. If your partner manages to persuade you to talk dirty to her, it is important to agree the boundaries to such talk, as adlibbing in the bedroom is full of grave pitfalls for the unwary (*see also* **Mistakes (sexual)**).

You are in bed with your new girlfriend.
SHE: *(looking over her shoulder) (puff)* You're the greatest.
YOU: *(blushing)* Really? *(wheeze)*
SHE: You bet.
YOU: *(puff)* Thanks. *(cough)*
You go to kiss her. You can't reach. You both collapse in a heap, laughing. Isn't life crazy?
YOU: Shall we change positions?
SHE: Sure.

You do that sort of judo turn that you think you invented, where you try to change positions whilst still remaining 'coupled'. It comes off. You feel chuffed. She is now beneath you.

SHE: Nice move.

YOU: *(bashful)* Thanks. It was nothing.

SHE: I can tell you're very experienced.

YOU: Oh well, you know. *(You look at your shoes, embarrassed, which is a neat trick because they're in the hall)*

SHE: *(hesitant)* So how about talking dirty to me?

YOU: *(taken aback)* What? I don't . . . I can't . . .

SHE: You don't have to. But *(she breathes deep into your ear)* I'd really like it if you did.

YOU: Stop it, that tickles!

To help things along, she playfully shoves her tongue deep into your ear. She immediately goes cross-eyed from the hit of earwax that she gets for her trouble. Mentally she notes to buy you some Q-tips.

YOU: *(squirming and mentally noting to cross off your ear-syringing appointment from your to-do list)* I'd rather . . .

SHE: *(trying to recover her mood)* Go on. Try it. It'll be fun.

YOU: *(hesitantly)* All right. *(Clearing your throat and looking her in the eye)* Here goes. Erm. *(With a polite yet firm thrust)* Take that, you dirty slut.

SHE: *(stopping suddenly)* Hey, who are you calling a slut?

YOU: What? I didn't mean . . . I thought that's what . . .

SHE: (*pushing you off*) How dare you.

YOU: I'm sorry.

She gets up, dresses and begins to leave.

YOU: (*to self*) Not again. (*To her*) Erm, you couldn't fill in a customer comment card for me on your way out, could you?

Texting (*see also* Multitasking, Phoning back, etc.)

As a modern dater you should equip yourself with a mobile phone, as texting is great for saucy flirting, arranging special rendezvous and generally keeping in touch with that special person who has taken your fancy. The alternative to which is, god forbid, actually TALKING to them.

Health Warning: Although for the most part texting is harmless fun, it does carry some associated health risks, namely:

- Texter's thumb – painful swelling caused by overuse of the thumb whilst tapping out messages on your phone keypad.
- Texter's nose – painful swelling caused by collision with stationary objects (lampposts, bus shelters, other texters) when not watching where you're walking due to tapping out messages on your phone keypad.
- Texter's cheek – painful swelling caused by a thunderous slap to the face when finally cornered by someone

you dumped by the cowardly method of tapping out a message on your phone keypad (possibly along the lines of: I h8 U. U make me ☹).

TIP If you want to get over a failed relationship more quickly, why not re-programme a humorous (to you, anyway) nickname for your ex-partner's number into your phone's memory, such as 'Liar', 'History', 'Death Breath' or 'Nobody Special'. Then all future texts and calls will be treated with the breezy contempt they deserve. (*See also* Answering the phone – to an ex.)

'The one'

That mythical person you are looking for. Don't be daunted by the fact that there are six billion people out there. Think about it. If you take out the too old, the too young, the already married, gay people (unless you *are* gay, in which case that would be silly), hermaphrodites, all the people who've already told you to sod off, the ones who can't make Rice crispie chocolate crackles, halitosis sufferers, the ones in prison and Cliff Richard, it only leaves about 1 billion to get through. Mind you, at 384,615* dates a week you might want to buy shares in Interflora, Gold Spot and Abra-kebab-ra (you can't afford to be too extravagant).

*1 billion divided by 2,600 (52 weeks × 50 yrs). Off you go!

Toothbrush sharing (after a one-night stand)

Not advisable. Nor should you secretly use her flatmate's brush and then dry it off so they don't notice.

Thoughtfulness

When tackling a sensitive issue with a new partner (their appearance, for instance), the word here is 'tact'. Try these handy responses to those common questions we all get asked:

- Is my breath very bad? *Not at all. It helps me find you in the dark.*
- Do you think my hands are too small? *No, I love them, they make my 'manhood' look bigger.*
- Would you say my nose is too big? *Of course not. I wish I could smoke a cigarette in the shower.*
- Do you think my bikini line needs waxing? *No. I like the fact that your legs have got sideburns.*

Trivial Pursuits

One of those games you will find yourself playing if you make the mistake of going round to your date's house to get ready for a night out. Other classics include: 'Guess my Weight', 'Where are my Shoes?' and whatever that game is called where you're just on your way out the door, she says she's forgotten something and then ten minutes later she comes down in a completely different bloody outfit.

You are upstairs pursuing the very important business of making you both late.

SHE: (*shouting*) Hurry up.

YOU: I am. (*You stop reading the magazine you'd found under her bed and start towelling your hair.*)

SHE: Oh, and can you bring down my coat?

YOU: (*to self*) The cheek of it. Telling me to hurry up. She's not even ready herself. Coat indeed (*grumble grumble*).

SHE: (*shouting*) Pardon?

YOU: Which one, darling?

SHE: My nice one.

YOU: (*to self*) That narrows it down a bit.

SHE: (*shouting*) Pardon?

YOU: Which nice one, love?

SHE: (*getting impatient at talking to an imbecile*) The black one.

YOU: They're all black.

SHE: The one I got for the wedding.

YOU: These are rubbish clues.

SHE: The one I was wearing (*then, mischievously*) when you *first met me.*

YOU: (*to self*) Here we go.

SHE: (*coming up the stairs*) You do remember what I was wearing when we first met, don't you?

YOU: I'm not playing any 'first time we met' games again. I got a black eye the last time.

SHE: You deserved it. What was I wearing?

YOU: Clothes?

SHE: Yes, but which ones?

YOU: Exactly! You don't know yourself.

SHE: Oh, yes I do. Go on, guess.

YOU: Is this for pie?

SHE: You don't remember. Oh, that's so hurtful.

YOU: It's not hurtful, it's normal. Give me a clue.

SHE: (*with unerring logic*) If you don't remember that means you don't love me.

YOU: Oh, stop it.

SHE: Okay, it's the same coat I wore to the restaurant last week.

YOU: Look, I don't know it. And anyway I was too distracted by your giant pepper-grinder gag. 'Manage it', indeed.

SHE: (*not letting you off that easily*) The coat I wore to the beach, that time when I wasn't wearing any (*now all coquettish*) *you know* . . . underwear (*giggle*).

YOU: Oh *that* one! Why didn't you say? (*Pause*) Doesn't it need dry cleaning?

'Truth or dare'

The game where you ask each other how many sexual partners you've had, and one of you says, 'tell the truth' and the other doesn't know if they dare.

> **TIP** When asked how many people you've slept with, don't say in an unguarded (drunk) moment 'Not enough'.

U

Underpant fairy (*see also* Washing-up pixie, Sock gnome, Tea elf)

That magical, mystery creature that used to pick up all your dirty underwear off the floor, then wash, dry and fold it neatly before putting it away in the chest of drawers. Sadly seems to have passed away since your ex moved out.

Undressing (*see also* Spontaneity)

When removing your pulling gear in front of a new partner after a successful night out (at last! hurrah!), there is a strict and proper procedure you should always follow. This is to maintain an attractive vision for her and so maximise your chances of getting past first base (when up till now you haven't even been allowed to get your bat out).

The correct order is:

1. Traffic cone (always first).
2. Tie (feel free to lick any 'Bombay Mix' off it for extra sustenance for the long night ahead).

3. Jacket (unless you've lost it already or taken it off to play drunken bullfighting).
4. Shirt (hopefully there will still be a few buttons done up so you can achieve your alluring eyeball to eyeball 'you lucky cow' countenance).
5. Shoes (sandals, flip flops, wellies, whatever).
6. Socks (make sure you get to the holey one first. If they are both holey, then go for the one with the biggest hole. If both have large holes, then go for the one that covers your least yellowy toenail).
7. Trousers (try to avoid thinking that speed is of the essence from now on, 'in case she changes her mind').
8. Truss (optional stage).
9. And finally – underpants.

If you feel like it, you might want to pause at this juncture and take a moody look out of the window to build the sexual tension, unless of course you've just remembered you are sporting a pair of *her* pants stolen from the washing line, in which case throw them out the window and quickly slide under the duvet saying 'Isn't it freezing? Okay if we turn out the light? I'm a bit, you know . . . shy.'

Problems arise when you perform the above procedure out of sequence and get down to the ocular feast that is you, standing there, in your socks and vest. Combine this with an unsightly, proud 'member' swaying around, knocking over candles and scaring the cat, and you will put any forthcoming sexual relations in jeopardy, regardless of how delicious the chips were that you bought her on the way home.

As far as men are concerned women may take their clothes off in any order they like, so long as they do it . . . *slowly*.

'Used to'

Although it's good to be considerate in a relationship, if you are *too* thoughtful you run the risk of storing up needless woe for yourself in the future. As your courtship efforts inevitably peter out you will be left with a disgruntled partner who torments you with: 'Remember when you **used to** tell me you loved me all the time?' 'Remember when you **used to** let *me* steer and *you* pushed the car?' 'Remember when you **used to** wash?'

In the same way you might find yourself harassing your partner with remarks like: 'Remember when you **used to** make me tea in the morning?' 'Remember when you **used to** come to bed wearing *fewer* clothes?' 'Remember when you **used to** smile?'

Uses for the stuff s/he left behind:

- 'Scrunchy' – sweat band for a small dog.
- Moisturiser – bicycle chain oil.
- Toner – emergency alcoholic component for a 'B52'.
- Old thongs – anti-pollution mask for a pervert.
- Photos of happier times – images for a novelty 'Guard Dog' warning sign.

- Bowl of pot pourri – kindling/ashtray.
- Sanitary products – aids for mopping up any mystery blue liquids you might spill.
- Emery boards – fake love-bite making tools.
- Cotton balls – snowballs to entertain small children.
- Shell-shaped soaps – party tongue-twister.
- Shoe horn – pizza server.
- Bitter memories – template for how *not* to behave next time.
- Broken dreams – anti-sleep aid for long car journeys.

V

Vacuuming

If you have decided – against the advice of this book – to bring a woman home (*see* **Inviting someone back to your flat**), then you will need to give the place a bit of a clean. You may find the standard home vacuum cleaner is too limited for your needs as the sucking nozzle is often too small to get bottles and cans through. In which case, why not invest in one of those Black and Decker industrial garden jobs? Then just open all the windows and set it to blow.

> **NOTE** You may also want to reconsider the practice of lazily vacuuming up loose coins, when we both know you will be retrieving them from that bag of hairy grey dust for milk money and bus fares later on in the month.

Valentine's Day

St Valentine: patron saint of rose growers, restaurant owners and divorce lawyers.

Vermin

The name you have decided to use when referring to that bloke from the darts team who ran off with your ex.

Voices (in your head)

Once you've been living alone for a while, you may be lucky enough to experience some of the more interesting tricks and surprises your brain has to offer. To avoid any embarrassment when hearing strange voices (for example, at a party, out shopping or on a packed bus) why not fit a 'hands free' mobile phone earpiece into your ear? You can then easily pass off any disturbed mutterings as a simple conversation (albeit regarding which sections of the government are out to get you) with someone from your packed social schedule.

Walks in the park

One of the more underrated aspects of being single and going out on dates is the opportunity this gives you to try things you wouldn't normally bother doing (*see also* **Changing your bed sheets**, **Flossing**, etc.). Taking a new date for a stroll in the local park is one such example, and it also gives you plenty of chances to show off your kind nature. However, if being spontaneously pleasant isn't something that comes naturally to you, I would advise you to rehearse thoroughly beforehand, or you could end up running into difficulties.

YOU: So, darling, would you like to go for a walk before dinner?

SHE: That would be nice. Where should we go?

YOU: To the park?

SHE: Okay, lead the way.

YOU: (*walking*) Hello, little child. (*You ruffle the child's hair, he starts to cry. You move away quickly.*) (*To her*) I love kids. I was in charge of the music for pass-the-parcel once. It was great seeing such joy on their little faces.

SHE: That's nice. A lot of men don't feel that way.

YOU: Not me. Although I don't like it when you turn the light on and they all scurry off.

SHE: Isn't that cockroaches?

YOU: Oh yeah. (*Changing the subject*) Hey look, a pigeon. Hello little pigeon. Ahh, he's looking for food. He thinks that cigarette butt is a crumb. Shall we see if he tries to peck it again? (*To the pigeon, in a childish voice*) Don't eat that Mr Pigeon, it's not proper food.

SHE: Flying rats, if you ask me.

YOU: (*backing off immediately*) And me. What an idiot. Look, he's got a limp. Bugger off, you. You're putting that limp on to make us feel sorry for you. (*To her*) Bloody scrounger.

A rough-looking individual approaches holding a magazine.

HOMELESS PERSON: *Big Issue*, mate?

YOU: Get stuff . . . Er, yes please. (*To her*) I always like to give what I can to tramps.

SHE: Good for you.

YOU: Although you're not allowed to call them that anymore, they're very sensitive. You've got to call them 'homeless beggars'. Or something like that.

SHE: You're so kind.

YOU: I know.

You reach into your pocket and try to identify a single pound coin by weight and feel alone so you don't have to show him how much change you actually have. You hand the coin over.

HOMELESS PERSON: It's £1.20

YOU: (*curt*) That's all I've got.

HOMELESS PERSON: Go on then. This is my last copy.

YOU: (*backing away from his breath*) Oh, good. You can go home now then, can't you?

HOMELESS PERSON: (*becoming angry*) Very funny. Twat.

YOU: (*realisation dawning*) Oh, sorry. (*You lead her away briskly.*) I think it's time for that restaurant, love.

Watching TV (alone)

Click
YOU: Prat.

Click
YOU: Knobhead.

Click
YOU: Tosser.

Click
YOU: Idiot.

Click
YOU: Ah, the news. Hmm, she's new.

A few minutes later
Click
YOU: Fool.
Click
YOU: Slaphead.
Click
YOU: Not you again.
Click
YOU: Prat

Sometimes you just can't beat a night in front of the telly on your own.

Ways to make yourself attractive to the opposite sex (*see also* Winning the lottery)

WOMEN: Get a driving licence.
MEN: Get a girlfriend.

What do men want?

While some men crave money, respect and power over others, most would settle for the simple things in life like a nice home, the occasional holiday and a personality that large-breasted blonde women find irresistible.

.

What do women want?

That's easy – they want it all, with the possible exception of cellulite.

What do women need?
It is a sad fact of life that women really only require two things in life from men:

1) To get them pregnant.
2) To hold their hair out their face when they're being sick.

Why?

What strange phenomenon is at work when you see your ex for the first time since your break up, and she is fifty times better looking than you remember? Well, it's possible this wasn't a chance encounter:

Your ex and the 'Guard Dog' are getting ready to go out.

CHAPERONE: (*in a vinegary tone*) You do know *he's* going to be at this party we're going to, don't you?

SHE: (*dropping her mascara*) You're joking!

CHAPERONE: (*now full of importance*) No, I'm not. He is. I heard it from Elaine Fernley, who got it from his sister. Do you want to go somewhere else?

SHE: No way. (*Thinking evilly*) I've been waiting for this moment for a long time. I think it's time Mr 'I want to spend more time with my mates' sees exactly what he's been missing since he gave me the elbow. Fetch me the tightest top and the tiniest skirt I possess. Oh, and some glitter!

We hear an acidic chuckle from the Guard Dog as they set to work.

At the party:

YOU: (*to friends*) I just needed my own space. Don't get me wrong, she was a nice . . .

In the corner of your eye you spot a vision of stunning loveliness entering the room. It's her. She mingles (chatting with every bloke) and then as casually as she can in thigh-length boots comes over to you. You haven't taken your eyes off her.

YOU: (*regretting wearing the Afghan coat and your pyjama bottoms*) Er, hi. Long time no . . . You look . . . What hap . . . How come . . . Where've you been? You look amazing!

SHE: Oh, hello. I didn't know you were going to be here.

YOU: It's great to see you. I've been meaning to phone . . .

SHE: Have you? I wouldn't have been in anyway. Funny, you seem shorter than I remember. And didn't you have more hair? What have I been up to, did you ask? (*Not waiting for an answer*) Oh, loads. (*Settling in*) I've just come back from Goa with the girls. That's where I got the tan. D'you like it? You and I were going to go there, weren't we? That's right, but you went to Corfu with your mates instead. Still, never mind. I met this great Swedish guy there. It's nothing serious though, just sex. He's a fitness instructor. Great body. And his, *you know* (*she flashes her eyes to your crotch*) is so large. When he gets an erection, we both faint!

YOU: (*on your knees now*) Oh, well, as long as you're happy.

There is more sour cackling as the Guard Dog leads her away

SHE: Nice seeing you again. Do have fun with your mates, won't you?

Winning him back

Ways that ought to work but don't:

- Cutting up all his suits.
- Gripping hold of his ankle as he walks down the street, shouting 'But I distinctly remember you saying you'd love me *forever*'.
- Guzzling several packs of Tic Tacs disguised as paracetamol tablets and declaring (with fresh minty breath): 'If you don't want to be with me (sob), I don't want to live.'
- Developing a phantom pregnancy (that turns out to be a gluten intolerance).
- Running him over.

- Sleeping with his boss.
- Going blonde.

Equally for men, if you want to rekindle the flame of love at some later date, you will find you have created obstacles for yourself if you pursued any of the following tactics:

- Putting intimate pictures of her up on the Internet.
- Turning up in your underwear at her work, unshaven and red eyed, sobbing 'Come back to me, woman. I need you. You're my world.'
- Writing 'I'm watching you' in paint-stripper on her car.
- Anonymously sending round a procession of hearses to her elderly parents' house.
- Feigning a terminal illness (that somehow never progresses beyond a need to lie on the couch).
- Writing 'Deceased Slapper' on any of her mail sent to you in error.
- Buying a sports car.

Women's magazines

A useful source of insider information about the opposite sex (*see also* **Diaries**, **Underwear drawer**, **Dustbins**, etc.), although if you read too many you could start thinking all women are obsessed with Princess Diana (mind you, she was 'lovely') and learning how to cleanse and tone their way to better orgasms. These publications can be identified by the wild claims printed on the front such as:

- Change your curtains and lose weight!
- I thought I had stomach ache and out popped an 8lb baby – says Dave from Wolverhampton.
- Lunch in Paris, dinner in Rome, luggage in Acapulco.
- How to trap your man – secrets of the SAS.
- Heroin – the evil trade that zaps cellulite.
- Beat the Christmas blues – become a Jehovah's Witness.
- I'm dating Princess Diana – from beyond the grave.
- The sexiest swimwear ever – Clingfilm!

Men's magazines plough a similar furrow, but with slightly different front-page teasers:
- 8 ways to drink yourself into a 6-pack.
- Drive your woman wild in the bedroom – hide her slippers.
- Baldness cures – we road-test three guillotines.
- Penis enlargement – is it all just a fallacy?
- Real Bloke stories – I married a suicide bomber but she went off with someone else.
- 3 ways to tell a stitch from a heart attack.

TIP It has been suggested that by using images of unobtainable female perfection, women's magazines are putting unfair pressure on young women. If this is true for you, then why not try doing what men do when they find themselves in the same position? Whenever a man sees a good-looking male model in smart clothes staring out at him from a stylish magazine, he will simply remark 'Dickhead', and move on.

X

XXXs (a.k.a. Kisses)

As well as being a fun way to get the latest life-threatening diseases, kissing is a great way to find out whether you have that special connection with someone because, after all, 'that's where it is' (*see* '**The Shoop Shoop Song**'). It is vital, therefore, to get your kissing skills up to scratch. If you're not sure about your abilities, look out for these tell-tale observations from your date:

- Is my kissing too sloppy? *If your partner is moved to say: 'Last time I was kissed like that, she had a wet nose, a tail and her breath smelled of tennis balls,' then the answer is probably yes.*

- Is my kissing too spirited? *If your partner is moved to say: 'So, does my spleen pass the taste test?' then the answer is probably yes.*

- Is my kissing too passionless? *If your partner is moved to say: 'Well, that's enough practice. I think I'm ready to move on to a live one now,' then the answer is probably yes.*

- Is my kissing too unappealing? *If your partner is moved to say: 'Mmm. If I'm not very much mistaken, Parmesan cheese with a hint of sick,' then the answer is probably yes.*

X-ray vision

A friend's remarkable ability to see through your thin veneer of lies.

YOU: (*out of breath*) Sorry I'm late, what a journey. The train didn't arrive on time, then I couldn't get a cab, then the taxi driver didn't know where he was going. The traffic was terrible, the worst I've ever seen it. Nightmare. (*Deep sigh*) Still, I'm here now.

FRIEND: How awful for you. Now do you want to tell me what really happened?

YOU: (*without missing a beat*) I was watching the end of *Star Trek*.

FRIEND: That's all I wanted to know.

Y

Yippee

Your secret reaction to:

- I ought to warn you that I get aroused *very* easily.
- I'm afraid my psychotic pal with the prison tattoos who fancies you has lost your phone number.
- I get my pleasure from giving pleasure to others.
- My friend and I tossed for you and guess what, we both won.
- I've got no sense of smell.

Young love (*see also* Love bites)

That carefree dating period, post puberty, when you thought it perfectly natural to:

- Kiss for hours, lips together, mouths open, no tongues, doing that odd smoke-ring blowing action until lock jaw set in.
- Show everyone you're 'an item' by walking side by side, arms wrapped tightly around each other's waist for weeks as if competing in some bizarre three-legged endurance race.

- Go out with three separate people in a lunch break.
- Finish with someone because they burped.
- Think that the ultimate declaration of love is when you're walking down the street together and she puts her hand in your back pocket.
- Let a girl know you fancy her by kicking her up the bum.
- 'Prove' you were going out with someone by letting any doubters smell your fingers.

Yucca

Scrawny tropical plant that sits in the corner of the lounge, totally unloved and un-watered, until the relationship ends, when it suddenly becomes the centre of a prolonged and bitter custody battle. (*See also* **Your jumpers, Her CDs, Am I being petty?**)

Z

Zealousness (Over-)

Be careful not to show excessive interest in your new part-ner's life, especially during the early days of the relationship (*see also* '**Used to**'). Remember, you're a bloke; you're not supposed to be *that* keen. There is a thin line between healthy attention and downright creepiness. You will raise her suspicions and possibly drive her away forever if you look deep into her eyes and say in a sincere voice things like:

- Please tell me about your cat's operation again.
- Really, your mum did all that with a leg of lamb?
- No, don't close the toilet door, I want to share *everything* with you.
- I'd be honoured to come shopping for an engagement present for your niece/sister/whoever.
- Tell me, what is it that makes *you* happy?
- I wish I could have your periods for you.

Zero

The chances of getting her in the sack on a date if:

- You're caught secretly using money-saving coupons to pay for anything.
- You turn up in a sarong and sandals outside of a recognised foreign holiday location.
- She catches you telling your friends that she's 'in the bag'.
- You get beaten in a fist fight – by a waitress.
- At any point you are sick out of your nose.
- You engage in foreplay after chopping chillies.
- You remark upon entering your flat: 'You'll have to keep your voice down, the wife's asleep in the other room.'
- You answered 'Yes' to any of the questions under **No** (except maybe the one about the Rolo).

Zero

The chances of not getting *him* in the sack.

Zinc

The element needed to maintain good sexual function. Found in oysters and tin baths.

Zones (erogenous)

The areas of the body which, when stimulated, increase sexual desire. Gentle stroking around the neck, breasts, thighs and feet should do it – and if you can do all four at once, get an agent.

Zoos

Quite possibly the perfect place to go on a date (*see also* **Budget dating**). Next to all that drooling, spitting, scrotum snuffling and belching, not to mention impressive minute-and-a-half sustained farting, you can't help but look like a pretty good catch.

Acknowledgements

Huge thanks go to Nick Herrett for his help in writing this book. To Liz Anstee for her invaluable feedback. And, as always, thanks to Antonia, Addison, Joe, Danny and Jon.

Especial thanks to all the women who dumped me, without whose selfless sacrifice this book could never have been written. God bless you.

THE A–Z OF
LIVING TOGETHER
A Survival Guide

Jeff Green
With a foreword by Jo Brand

What happens when those two most incompatible of creatures – the human male and the human female – settle down for a life of togetherness and arguments about the toilet seat? Award-winning comedian Jeff Green bravely sets out to discover the truth. Why is 'Wow, you're a fantastic cleaner' not considered a compliment? And what *is* it about women and candles . . . ?

Along the way he offers

- helpful advice: why you shouldn't cheer when your partner says, 'I'm not angry, I'm disappointed'
- handy tips: ways to avoid becoming broody – get up every hour throughout the night and burn £200
- and essential buys: see exercise equipment and other places to hang wet washing'.

Whether you're hopelessly coupled or blissfully single, *The A-Z of Living Together* has all the answers you need. Because it's not just men who behave badly . . .

'One of Britain's very best observational comics'
Guardian